SPEA

MALAY

IBRAHIM ISMAIL

GOLDEN BOOKS CENTRE SDN. BHD.
KUALA LUMPUR

GOLDEN BOOKS CENTRE SDN. BHD., [T-142884]
Lot 4.1, 4th Floor, WISMA SHEN,
149, Jalan Masjid India,
50100 Kuala Lumpur.
Tel: 03-2939862/2939864/2931661/2933661
Fax: 03-2928035
E-mail: gbc@pc.jaring.my

© IBRAHIM ISMAIL
  First Published: 1991
  Reprinted: 1992, 1993, 1994, 1996, 1997, 2000

Member of the Malaysian Book Publishers Association
Membership Number: 8208

Code: RP7-20-200420

Printed by: Syarikat Percetakan Ihsan, Selangor D.E.

ISBN: 967-9959-53-8

PUBLISHER'S NOTE

This book is designed for those who want to master Bahasa Malaysia within the shortest possible time with or without a teacher. The book consists of practical sentence patterns, a simple explanation of Malaysian orthography, an appendix with conjugation charts and a Bahasa Malaysia-English vocabulary.

The main part of the book presents all basic sentence patterns of colloquial Bahasa Malaysia. The vocabulary is strictly selected and the material is brought together in the form of practical dialogues.

In learning a foreign language the first step should be to get yourself accustomed to hearing the spoken language by your teacher or a native speaker. Then you must master the sound system to enable you to understand the meaning of speech sounds. Now you have to master a selected range of the most essential sentence patterns with a limited vocabulary.

Our organs of speech are accustomed to pronouncing our native language since our infancy. It is this very fact that makes it hard for us to learn a new language. The only effective way to overcome this difficulty is by doing oral drills as much as possible. We should regularly and repeatedly mimick and drill the stream of speech sound, no matter how strange it may be. Even an infant can acquire the habit of speaking unconsciously just by mimicking and drilling the speech sounds of his parents. Gradually he becomes a good speaker and finally can speak with the best pronunciation.

Thus, in other words, the most effective way to learn a new language is by listening, imitating, speaking and more speaking. By doing so the speech sounds as well as the basic sentence patterns will become part of your mental habit. It will be better, if you learn the sentence patterns by heart. Then after two or three weeks you will be able to understand Bahasa Malaysia and make yourself understood when Malaysians speak to you.

Good luck!

CONTENTS/KANDUNGAN

Page/Muka Surat

Publisher's Note
The Phonetic System
The First Lesson/**Pelajaran Pertama**
Names, Forms Of Address And Nationalities (I)
Nama, Panggilan Dan Bangsa (I) 1

The Second Lesson/**Pelajaran Kedua**
Names, Forms Of Address And Nationalities (II)
Nama, Panggilan Dan Bangsa (II) 2

The Third Lesson/**Pelajaran Ketiga**
Names, Forms Of Address And Nationalities (III)
Nama, Panggilan Dan Bangsa (III) 3

The Fourth Lesson/**Pelajaran Keempat**
Names, Forms Of Address And Nationalities (IV)
Nama, Panggilan Dan Bangsa (IV) 4

The Fifth Lesson/**Pelajaran Kelima**
Occupations (I)/**Pekerjaan (I)** 5

The Sixth Lesson/**Pelajaran Keenam**
Occupations (II)/**Pekerjaan (II)** 6

The Seventh Lesson/**Pelajaran Ketujuh**
Demonstrative Pronouns/**Kata Penunjuk Benda** 7

The Eighth Lesson/**Pelajaran Kelapan**
What's This? What's That? (I)/**Apa Ini? Apa Itu? (I)** 8

The Ninth Lesson/**Pelajaran Kesembilan**
What's This? What's That (II)/**Apa Ini? Apa Itu? (II)** 9

The Tenth Lesson/**Pelajaran Kesepuluh**
What's That? (Names Of Places)/**Apakah Itu? (Nama-Nama Tempat)** 10

The Eleventh Lesson/**Pelajaran Kesebelas**
Where? (Names Of Places)/**Di Mana? (Nama Tempat)** 11

The Twelfth Lesson/**Pelajaran Kedua Belas**
Which One?/**Yang Mana?** 12

The Thirteenth Lesson/**Pelajaran Ketiga Belas**
Where? (Instrument)/**Di Mana? (Alatan)** 13

The Fourteenth Lesson/**Pelajaran Keempat Belas**
Stationery, Etc./**Alat Tulis Dan Lain-Lain** 13

The Fifteenth Lesson/**Pelajaran Kelima Belas**
Possesions/**Kepunyaan** 14

The Sixteenth Lesson/**Pelajaran Keenam Belas**
Shoes Etc./**Kasut Dan Lain-Lain** 15

The Seventeenth Lesson/**Pelajaran Ketujuh Belas**
Cigarettes & Lighter/**Rokok Dan Pemetik Api/Mancis**. 16

The Eighteenth Lesson/**Pelajaran Kelapan Belas**
Rooms/**Bilik** 17

The Nineteenth Lesson/**Pelajaran Kesembilan Belas**
Directions/**Nama Arah** 18

The Twentieth Lesson/**Pelajaran Kedua Puluh**
Things (I)/**Benda-Benda (II)** 19

The Twenty First Lesson/**Pelajaran Kedua Puluh Satu**
Bedroom/**Bilik Tidur** 20

The Twenty Second Lesson/**Pelajaran Kedua Puluh Dua**
Things (II)/**Benda-Benda (II)** 21

The Twenty-Third Lesson/**Pelajaran Kedua Puluh Tiga**
Possession/**Kepunyaan** 22

The Twenty Fourth Lesson/**Pelajaran Kedua Puluh Empat**
At Home/**Suasana Di Rumah** 23

The Twenty Fifth Lesson/**Pelajaran Kedua Puluh Lima**
Hotel, Etc./**Hotel Dan Sebagainya** 24

The Twenty Sixth Lesson/**Pelajaran Kedua Puluh Enam**
Yours And His/**Kepunyaan Anda Dan Dia** 26

The Twenty Seventh Lesson/**Pelajaran Kedua Puluh Tujuh**
Town Hall Etc/**Dewan Orang Ramai Dan Lain-Lain** 27

The Twenty Eighth Lesson/**Pelajaran Kedua Puluh Lapan**
Zoo, Etc/**Zoo Dan Lain-Lain** 28

The Twenty Ninth Lesson/**Pelajaran Kedua Puluh Sembilan**
Counting (I)/**Mengira (I)** 29

The Thirtieth Lesson/**Pelajaran Ketiga Puluh**
Counting (II)/**Mengira (II)** 30

The Thirty-First Lesson/**Pelajaran Ketiga Puluh Satu**
Counting (III)/**Mengira (III)** 31

The Thirty Second Lesson/**Pelajaran Ketiga Puluh Dua**
Counting People And Animals/**Mengira Orang Dan Haiwan** . 32

The Thirty-Third Lesson/**Pelajaran Ketiga Puluh Tiga**
Counting Things/**Mengira Benda** 34

The Thirty Fourth Lesson/**Pelajaran Ketiga Puluh Empat**
Arithmetic/**Kira-Kira** 35

The Thirty-Fifth Lesson/**Pelajaran Ketiga Puluh Lima**
Hotel/**Hotel** 36

The Thirty-Sixth Lesson/**Pelajaran Ketiga Puluh Enam**
Fraction/**Nombor Pecahan** 37

The Thirty-Seventh Lesson/**Pelajaran Ketiga Puluh Tujuh**
Jobs (I)/**Pekerjaan (I)** 39

The Thirty-Eight Lesson/**Pelajaran Ketiga Puluh Lapan**
Jobs (II)/**Pekerjaan (II)** 40

The Thirty-Ninth Lesson/**Pelajaran Ketiga Puluh Sembilan**
Money (I)/**Wang (I)** 41

The Fortieth Lesson/**Pelajaran Keempat Puluh**
Prices (I)/**Harga (I)** 42

The Forty-First Lesson/**Pelajaran Keempat Puluh Satu**
Prices (II)/**Harga (II)** 43

The Forty-Second Lesson/**Pelajaran Keempat Puluh Dua**
Money (II)/**Wang (II)** 44

The Forty-Third Lesson/**Pelajaran Keempat Puluh Tiga**
Drink, Beverages/**Minuman** 45

The Forty-Fourth Lesson/**Pelajaran Keempat Puluh Empat**
Prices of Food (I)/**Harga Makanan (I)** 46

The Forty-Fifth Lesson/**Pelajaran Keempat Puluh Lima**
Prices Of Food (II)/**Harga Makanan (II)** 47

The Forty Sixth Lesson/**Pelajaran Keempat Puluh Enam**
Pickpockets/**Penyeluk Saku** 48

The Forty-Seventh Lesson/**Pelajaran Keempat Puluh Tujuh**
Department Store (I)/**Kedai Serbanika (I)** 49

The Forty-Eighth Lesson/**Pelajaran Keempat Puluh Lapan**
Department Store (II)/**Kedai Serbanika (II)** 51

The Forty-Ninth Lesson/**Pelajaran Keempat Puluh Sembilan**
Size Of Clothes/**Ukuran Pakaian** 52

The Fiftieth Lesson/**Pelajaran Kelima Puluh**
Bargaining/**Tawar Menawar** 53

Fifty-First Lesson/**Pelajaran Kelima Puluh Satu**
Shopping (I)/**Membeli-Belah (I)** 54

Fifty Second Lesson/**Pelajaran Kelima Puluh Dua**
Shopping (II)/**Membeli-Belah (II)** 55

Fifty Third Lesson/**Pelajaran Kelima Puluh Tiga**
Shopping (III)/**Membeli-Belah (III)** 56

Fifty-Fourth Lesson/**Pelajaran Kelima Puluh Empat**
Shopping (IV)/**Membeli-Belah (IV)** 57

Fifty-Fifth Lesson/**Pelajaran Kelima Puluh Lima**
Weather (I)/**Cuaca (I)** 59

Fifty-Sixth Lesson/**Pelajaran Kelima Puluh Enam**
Weather (II)/**Cuaca (II)** 60

Fifty-Seventh Lesson/**Pelajaran Kelima Puluh Tujuh**
Weather (III)/**Cuaca (III)** 61

Fifty-Eight Lesson/**Pelajaran Kelima Puluh Lapan**
Weather (IV)/**Cuaca (IV)** 62

The Fifty-Ninth Lesson/**Pelajaran Kelima Puluh Sembilan**
Weather (V)/**Cuaca (IV)** 63

Sixtieth Lesson/**Pelajaran Keenam Puluh**
Dates (I)/**Haribulan (I)** 64

The Sixty-First Lesson/**Pelajaran Keenam Puluh Satu**
Vacation, Holiday/**Hari Cuti** 65

Sixty-Second Lesson/**Pelajaran Keenam Puluh Dua**
Months Of The Year/**Bulan** 66

Sixty-Third Lesson/**Pelajaran Keenam Puluh Tiga**
Seasons/**Musim** 67

Sixty-Fourth Lesson/**Pelajaran Keenam Puluh Empat**
Dates (II)/**Haribulan (II)** 68

Sixty-Fifth Lesson/**Pelajaran Keenam Puluh Lima**
Dates (III)/**Haribulan (III)** 69

Sixty-Sixth Lesson/**Pelajaran Keenam Puluh Enam**
Independence Day/**Hari Kemerdekaan** 70

Sixty-Seventh Lesson/**Pelajaran Keenam Puluh Tujuh**
Birthday/**Hari Jadi** 71

Sixty-Eighth Lesson/**Pelajaran Keenam Puluh Lapan**
Itinerary/**Jadual Perjalanan** 73

Sixty-Ninth Lesson/**Pelajaran Keenam Puluh Sembilan**
Food In The Restaurant/**Makanan Di Restoran** 74

Seventy-First Lesson/**Pelajaran Ketujuh Puluh Satu**
Travel (I)/**Melancong (I)** 75

Seventy-Second Lesson/**Pelajaran Ketujuh Puluh Dua**
Travel (II)/**Melancong (II)** 76

Seventy-Third Lesson/**Pelajaran Ketujuh Puluh Tiga**
Pleasure (I) – Bali/**Hiburan (I) – Bali** 78

Seventy-Fourth Lesson/**Pelajaran Ketujuh Puluh Empat**
Pleasure (II) – Bali/**Hiburan (II) – Bali** 79

Seventh-Fifth Lesson/**Pelajaran Ketujuh Puluh Lima**
Comparison (I)/**Perbandingan (I)** 80

Seventy-Sixth Lesson/**Pelajaran Ketujuh Puluh Enam**
Comparison (II)/**Perbandingan (II)**   82

Seventy-Seventh Lesson/**Pelajaran Ketujuh Puluh Tujuh**
Living/**Tempat Tinggal**   83

Seventy-Eighth Lesson/**Pelajaran Ketujuh Puluh Lapan**
Places Of Interest/**Tempat-Tempat Yang Menarik**   84

Seventy-Ninth Lesson/**Pelajaran Ketujuh Puluh Sembilan**
Visiting (I)/**Melawat (I)**   86

Eightieth Lesson/**Pelajaran Kelapan Puluh**
Visiting (II)/**Melawat (II)**   87

The Eighty-First Lesson/**Pelajaran Kelapan Puluh Satu**
Taxi (I)/**Teksi (I)**   88

Eighty-Second Lesson/**Pelajaran Kelapan Puluh Dua**
Taxi (II)/**Teksi (II)**   89

The Eighty-Third Lesson/**Pelajaran Kelapan Puluh Tiga**
Shows (I)/**Pertunjukan (I)**   90

Eighty-Fourth Lesson/**Pelajaran Kelapan Puluh Empat**
Shows (II)/**Pertunjukan (II)**   92

Eighty-Fifth Lesson/**Pelajaran Kelapan Puluh Lima**
Trip/**Perjalanan**   93

Eighty-Sixth Lesson/**Pelajaran Kelapan Puluh Enam**
On The Plane/**Dalam Kapalterbang**   94

Eighty-Seventh Lesson/**Pelajaran Kelapan Puluh Tujuh**
Being Ill/**Sakit**   95

Eighty-Eighth Lesson/**Pelajaran Lapan Puluh Lapan**
Plan/**Rancangan**   96

The Eighty-Ninth Lesson/**Pelajaran Kelapan Puluh Sembilan**
Although/**Meskipun** 98

Ninetieth Lesson/**Pelajaran Kesembilan Puluh**
Disjunctive Sentences/**Ayat Pertentangan** 99

Ninety First Lesson/**Pelajaran Kesembilan Puluh Satu**
Courtesies (I)/**Berbudi Bahasa (I)** 100

Ninety-Second Lesson/**Pelajaran Kesembilan Puluh Dua**
Courtesis (II)/**Berbudi Bahasa (II)** 101

Ninety-Third Lesson/**Pelajaran Kesembilan Puluh Tiga**
Favourites/**Kesukaan** 102

Ninety-Fourth Lesson/**Pelajaran Kesembilan Puluh Empat**
Passive Sentences (I)/**Ayat Pasif (I)** 104

Ninety-Fifth Lesson/**Pelajaran Kesembilan Puluh Lima**
Borrowing Money/**Meminjam Wang** 105

Ninety-Sixth Lesson/**Pelajaran Kesembilan Puluh Enam**
Passive Sentences/**Ayat Pasif (II)** 106

Ninety-Seventh Lesson/**Pelajaran Kesembilan Puluh Tujuh**
Use Of Prepositions/**Penggunaan Kata Depan (I)** 108

Ninety-Eighth Lesson/**Pelajaran Kesembilan Puluh Lapan**
Use Of Prepositions/**Penggunaan Kata Depan (II)** 109

Ninety-Ninth Lesson/**Pelajaran Kesembilan Puluh Sembilan**
Time/**Waktu** 110

One Hundreth Lesson/**Pelajaran Keseratus**
Phrases (I)/**Ungkapan-Ungkapan (I)** 111

One Hundred And First Lesson/**Pelajaran Keseratus Satu**
Phrases (II)/**Ungkapan-Ungkapan (II)** 112

One Hundred And Second Lesson/**Pelajaran Keseratus Dua**
Phrases (III)/**Ungkapan-Ungkapan (III)** 113

Compounds (I)/**Kata Majmuk (I)** 114

Compounds (II)/**Kata Majmuk (II)** 114

Adverbs (I)/**Kata Keterangan (I)** 115

Adverbs (II)/**Kata Keterangan (II)** 116

Passive Sentences (I)/**Ayat Pasif (I)** 117

Passive Sentences (II)/**Ayat Pasif (II)** 118

Passive Sentences (III)/**Ayat Pasif (III)** 119

The "Key to Pronounciation" provided below will be helpful in pronouncing the Bahasa Malaysia words.

THE PHONETIC SYSTEM

VOWELS
a e i o u

DIPHTHONGS
ai, au, oi

CONSONANTS
b, c, d, f, g, h, j, k, l, m, n, p, q, r, s, t, v, w, y, z.

VOWEL SOUNDS

a   In open syllables "a" is pronounced like "a" in "father", e.g. ada (be, exist), dada (chest), apa (what), kata (word).

In close syllables the "a" sound is shorter as "u" in "cut", e.g. lambat (slow), dapat (to get), makan (to eat).

e   There are two kinds of "e", stressed and unstressed "e". The stressed "e" used to have a stressed mark "e", but in modern spelling such a mark has been omitted.

In open syllables the stressed "e" is pronounced like "e" in "very", "every", e.g. perak (silver), beta (I), kereta (a car).

In close syllables the stressed "e" is pronounced like "e" in "bed", e.g. sen (a cent).

i

i In open syllables "i" is pronounced like "ee" in "feet", e.g. ini (this), kini (now), makcik (aunt), pipi (cheek).

In closed syllables it is pronounced as "i" in "thin", e.g. main (to play), baik (good).

o In open syllables "o" is pronounced like "o" in "body" or story", e.g. roti (bread), boleh (allowed to, may).

In closed syllables it is pronounced just in the same way as in the open syllables, eg. ombak (wave), pokok (tree).

u In open syllables it is pronounced like "oo" in "food" (u:). The vowel is slightly longer, e.g. bulan (moon), itu (that).

In closed syllables it is pronounced like "u" in "put", e.g. rumput (grass), kabut (fog), untuk (for), mulut (mouth), urut (massage), duduk (to sit), undangan (invitation).

DIPHTHONGS

ai "ai" is pronounced like "i" in "I", "like", "kite", etc. e.g. ramai (crowded), damai (peaceful), pantai (shore), landai (slope).

N.B. "ai" in "baik" (good) and "lain" (other) is not a diphthong. These words are pronounced "ba-ik", "la-in".

au It is roughly equivalent to "ow" in "now", "cow"

etc. e.g. kerbau (buffalo), kalau (if), danau (lake), pulau (island).

N.B. But "au" in laut (sea) and mahu (will) is not a diphthong. These words are pronounced "la-ut" and "ma-hu".

oi This diphthong is pronounced like "oy" in "boy", "toy" etc. e.g. amboi (well), koboi (a cowboy).

CONSONANTS

In general the pronunciation of Malaysian consonants is quite similar to that of English, but Malaysians consonants are generally softer and not aspirated.

b is pronounced like "b" in "rub" or "b" in "back" but much softer, e.g. baru (new), sebab (reason).

c is pronounced like "ch" in "church", e.g. cinta (love), cicak (lizard), cucu (grandchild).

d is pronouced like "d" in "red", e.g. dada (chest), duda (widower), mendidik (to educate).

g is pronounced like "g" in "dog", "good" etc. e.g. gugup (nervous), gigi (tooth), agak (rather).

h is pronounced like "h" in "home", "hit", "hot", etc. e.g. hakim (judge), hujan (rain), basah (wet).

j   is pronounced like "j" in "job", "jack", etc. e.g. jalan (way), jelas (clear), jujur (honest).

f   is pronounced like "f" in "fine", "fat", "if", etc. e.g. keluarga (family), fasih (fluent in speaking).

k   is pronounced like "k" in "book", "kill", etc. e.g. kaki (foot, leg), kuku (nail), kaku (rigid).

l   is pronounced like "l" in "lily", "look", "tell", etc. e.g. lalu (to pass), kenal (to know).

m   is pronounced like "m" in "man", "dam", etc. e.g. malam (night), iklim (climate), makan (to eat).

n   is pronounced like "n" in "nine", "nun", "none", etc. e.g. nenas (pineapple), nenek (grandmother), anak (child), bunga (flower).

p   is pronounced lika "p", in "put", "pop", etc. e.g. asap (smoke), pipi (cheek).

q   is pronounced like "q" in "question", "quality", etc. e.g. Al-Quran (The Koran), taufiq (God's favour).

r   is pronounced like "r" in "radio", "run", "rot", etc. e.g. rumah (home, house), akar (root), lalat (fly), bubur (porridge), ukur (to measure), etc.

s   is pronounced like "s" in "sit", "son", "sun", etc. e.g. saksi (witness), susu (milk), habis (finished).

t   is pronounced like "t" in "tan", "cut", "total", etc. e.g. surat (letter), tulis (write), tulus (sincere), tinta (ink), takut (fear), etc.

v   is pronounced like e.g. "television" (televisyen), "revolusi" and " subversive".

w   is pronounced like "w" in "will", "win" "won", etc. e.g. waktu (time), kewajipan (duty).

y   is pronounced like "y" in "yes", "yet", "you" etc. e.g. ya (yes), yang (that), yayasan (foundation), kayu (wood), kaya (rich).

ng is pronounced like "ng" in "king", "sing", "sting", e.g. mengapa (why), siang (daytime), malang (unfortunate), petang (afternoon), mengunyah (to chew), kucing (cat), anjing (dog) etc.

ny is pronounced like "ny" in "canyon", e.g. menyanyi (to sing), Puan (Mrs), menyalak (to bark).

sy is pronounced like "sh" in "should", "shy" etc. e.g. syukur (thanks to God), syarat (condition, term, requirement).

z   is pronounced like z in "zoo", "zone", etc. e.g. zaman (period, age), Aziz (name of male person).

No two persons can speak a language, with the same phonetic. This is very true in the case of Malaysians. Their pronounciation depends on the place of birth.

THE FIRST LESSON

NAMES, FORMS OF ADDRESS AND NATIONALITIES (I)

I am John Smith.
I am a teacher.
I am American.
I am a man.
Your name is Yamada.
Your name is Yamada.
Your are not a teacher.

You are a tourist.
You are Japanese.
You are not American.

My name is John Smith
I am not Japanese.
I am not a tourist.
My name is John Smith.

You are a man.

PELAJARAN PERTAMA

NAMA, PANGGILAN DAN BANGSA (I)

Saya John Smith.
Saya seorang guru.
Saya orang Amerika.
Saya seorang lelaki.
Encik bernama Yamada.
Nama Encik Yamada.
Encik bukan seorang guru.

Encik seorang pelancung.
Encik orang Jepun.
Encik bukan orang Amerika.

Nama saya John Smith.
Saya bukan orang Jepun.
Saya bukan pelancung.
Saya bernama John Smith.

Encik seorang lelaki.

THE SECOND LESSON

NAMES, FORMS OF ADDRESS AND NATIONALITIES (II)

You are Japanese.
My name is Watanabe.
I am Japanese, too.
Miss Hanako is Japanese, too.
Mr. Yamada and Miss Hanako are Japanese.
Mr. Green is British.

Mr. Green is not American.
I am Japanese and Mr. Smith is American.

Mr. Green is not Japanese.

Mr. Smith is not Japanese.

Mr. Green and Smith are not Japanese.
Mr. Watanabe is Japanese and Mr. Green is British.

Mr. Yamada and Watanabe are Japanese.

PELAJARAN KEDUA

NAMA, PANGGILAN DAN BANGSA (II)

Encik orang Jepun.
Nama saya Watanabe.
Saya juga orang Jepun.
Cik Hanako juga orang Jepun.
Encik Yamada dan Cik Hanako orang Jepun.
Encik Green orang Inggeris.

Encik Green bukan orang Amerika.
Saya orang Jepun dan Encik Smith orang Amerika.

Encik Green bukan orang Jepun.
Encik Smith bukan orang Jepun.

Encik Green dan Smith bukan orang Jepun.
Encik Watanabe orang Jepun dan Encik Green orang Inggeris.
Encik Yamada dan Watanabe orang Jepun.

2

NAMES, FORMS OF ADDRESS AND NATIONALITIES (III)

This is Mr. Sundoro.

Mr. Sundoro is Indonesian.

Mr. Sundoro is not Japanese.

Mr. Sundoro is a man.

That is Mrs. Sundoro.

Mrs. Sundoro is also Indonesian.

Mrs. Sundoro is a woman.

Mr. and Mrs. Sundoro are Indonesian.

They are not Japanese.

Mr. Kim is Chinese.

Mrs. Kim is Chinese, too.

This is Mr. Fokker.

Mr. Fokker is Dutch.

Mr. Fokker is a foreigner.

NAMA, PANGGILAN DAN BANGSA (III)

Ini Encik Sundoro.

Encik Sundoro orang Indonesia.

Encik Sundoro bukan orang Jepun.

Encik Sundoro orang lelaki.

Itu Puan Sundoro.

Puan Sundoro juga orang Indonesia.

Puan Sundoro seorang perempuan.

Encik dan Puan Sundoro orang Indonesia.

Mereka bukan orang Jepun.

Encik Kim orang Cina.

Puan Kim juga orang Cina.

Ini Encik Fokker.

Encik Fokker orang Belanda.

Encik Fokker orang asing.

3

Miss Hanako is a foreigner, too.	Cik Hanoko juga orang asing.

THE FOURTH LESSON

NAMES, FORMS OF ADDRESS AND NATIONALITIES (IV)

PELAJARAN KEEMPAT

NAMA, PANGGILAN DAN BANGSA (IV)

Mr. Afandi is not a foreigner.	Encik Afandi bukan orang asing.
Mrs. Afandi is not a foreigner, either.	Puan Afandi juga bukan orang asing.
They are not foreigners.	Mereka bukan orang asing.
They are Malaysian.	Mereka orang Malaysia.
Mr. Smith and Green are foreigners, too.	Encik Smith dan Green juga orang asing.
My name is Yamada and I am a foreigner.	Nama saya Yamada dan saya orang asing.
Mrs. Hugo is a Frenchwoman.	Puan Hugo orang Perancis.
Mr. Rizal is a Filipino.	Encik Rizal orang Filipina.
They are all foreigners.	Mereka semua orang asing.
I am a foreigner but you are a Malaysian.	Saya orang asing tetapi anda orang Malaysia.

Mrs. Yamada is a woman.	Puan Yamada seorang perempuan.
Miss Hanako is a girl.	Cik Hanako seorang gadis.
Mrs. Afandi and Mrs. Yamada are women.	Puan Afandi dan Puan Yamada orang perempuan.
They are women.	Mereka orang perempuan.
They are not men.	Mereka bukan orang lelaki.

THE FIFTH LESSON

OCCUPATIONS (I)

PELAJARAN KELIMA

PEKERJAAN (I)

Is that Mr. Yamada?	Encik Yamadakah itu?
Yes, that is Mr. Yamada.	Ya, itu Encik Yamada.
What is Mr. Yamada's nationality?	Apakah bangsa Encik Yamada?
Mr. Yamada is Japanese.	Encik Yamada orang Jepun.
Is Mr. Sundoro Japanese?	Adakah Encik Sundoro orang Jepun?
No. Mr. Sundoro is not Japanese.	Bukan, Encik Sundoro bukan orang Jepun.
Is Mr. Green American?	Apakah Encik Green orang Amerika?
No. Mr. Green is British.	Bukan, Encik Green orang Inggeris.

Is that man a teacher?
Yes, that man is a teacher.
Is Miss Hanako a merchant?
No, Miss Hanako is not a merchant.
She is a stewardess.
She is Japanese.
She lives in Tokyo.

Adakah orang itu guru?
Ya, orang itu guru.
Apakah Cik Hanako seorang saudagar?
Bukan, Cik Hanako bukan saudagar.
Dia peramugari.
Dia orang Jepun.
Dia tinggal di Tokyo.

THE SIXTH LESSON

OCCUPATIONS (II)

Who is that man?
That man is Mr. Smith.

Is he a businessmen?
No, he is not a businessman.
He is a teacher.
Where is he now?
He is at school.
Is Mrs. Salmah a teacher?

No, Mrs. Salmah is not a teacher.
She is a housewife.
She is at home now.

PELAJARAN KEENAM

PEKERJAAN (II)

Siapakah orang itu?
Orang itu ialah Encik Smith.

Pengusahakah dia?
Bukan, dia bukan pengusaha.
Dia guru.
Di mana dia sekarang?
Dia di sekolah.
Apakah Puan Salmah seorang guru?

Bukan, Puan Salmah bukan seorang guru.
Dia suri rumahtangga.
Dia sekarang di rumah.

Who is that man? | Siapakah lelaki itu?
He is Mr. Latif. | Itu Encik Latif.
He is a government servant. | Dia pegawai kerajaan.

I am a government servant too. | Saya juga pegawai kerajaan.

THE SEVENTH LESSON

DEMONSTRATIVE PRONOUNS

This is a book.
That is a magazine.
That is a newspaper.
Those are a magazine and newspaper.
This ia a briefcase.
These are a book and briefcase.
Is this a newspaper?
Yes, this is a newspaper.
Is that a newspaper too?
No, that is not a newspaper.
That is a calendar.
This is a cup and that is a saucer.

PELAJARAN KETUJUH

KATA PENUNJUK BENDA

Ini buku.
Itu majalah.
Itu suratkhabar.
Itu majalah dan suratkhabar.
Ini beg bimbit.
Ini buku dan beg bimbit.

Suratkhabarkah ini?
Ya, ini suratkhabar.
Suratkhabar jugakah itu?
Bukan, itu bukan suratkhabar.
Itu kalendar.
Ini cawan dan itu piring.

That is a glass and this is a teapot.	Itu gelas dan ini teko.
This is a table and that is a chair.	Ini meja dan itu kerusi.
That is a television and this is a radio.	Itu televisyen dan ini radio.

THE EIGHTH LESSON	PELAJARAN KELAPAN
WHAT'S THIS? **WHAT'S THAT? (I)**	**APA INI?** **APA ITU? (I)**

What is that?	Itu apa?
That is a tree.	Itu pokok.
What tree is that?	Pokok apa itu?
That is a coconut palm tree.	Itu pohon kelapa.
This is a bamboo tree.	Ini pokok buluh.
That is a banana tree.	Itu pokok pisang.
Is that a house?	Rumahkah itu?
No, that is not a house.	Bukan, itu bukan rumah.
Then, what is it?	Kalau begitu, apakah itu?
That is an office.	Itu pejabat.
What office is that?	Pejabat apakah itu?
That is a post office.	Itu pejabat pos.
That is not a house, but an office.	Itu bukan rumah, tetapi pejabat.
This is a house and that is a post office.	Ini rumah dan itu pejabat pos.

THE NINTH LESSON

WHAT'S THIS?
WHAT'S THAT (II)

What is this?
This is a machine.
What machine is this?
This is a typewriter.
Is that a typewriter too?
No, that is not a type-
writer.
Then what machine is
that?
That is a calculating
machine.
What machine is this?
This is a mimeograph.
That is a sewing machine.
That is not a washing
machine.
Is this a table?
No, this is a blackboard.
This is a blackboard and
that is chalk.

PELAJARAN
KESEMBILAN

APA INI?
APA ITU? (II)

Ini apa?
Ini mesin.
Mesin apa ini?
Ini mesin taip.
Mesin taip jugakah itu?
Bukan, itu bukan mesin
taip.
Kalau begitu, mesin apa-
kah itu?
Itu mesin kira.

Ini mesin apa?
Ini mesin stensil.
Itu mesin jahit.
Itu bukan mesin basuh.

Mejakah ini?
Bukan, ini papan hitam.
Ini papan hitam dan itu
kapur tulis.

9

THE TENTH LESSON

WHAT'S THAT?
(NAMES OF PLACES)

Is that an office?
No, that is a restaurant.
Is that a restaurant too?
No, this is a dormitory.
What office is that?
That is a post office.
Is that a hotel?
No, that is a cinema.

Is that a house?
No, that is Town Hall.

This is a hotel and that is
  a restaurant.
Those are the post office
  and the railways station.
What building is that?
That is a museum.
This is a mosque and that
  is a church.

PELAJARAN KESEPULUH
APAKAH ITU? (NAMA-NAMA TEMPAT)

Pejabatkah itu?
Bukan, itu restoran.
Restoran jugakah itu?
Bukan, ini asrama.
Pejabat apakah itu?
Itu pejabat pos.
Hotelkah itu?
Bukan, itu panggung wa-
  yang.
Rumahkah itu?
Bukan, itu Dewan Orang
  Ramai.
Ini hotel dan itu restoran.

Itu pejabat pos dan ste-
  sen keretapi.
Bangunan apa itu?
Itu muzium.
Ini masjid dan itu gereja.

THE ELEVENTH LESSON

WHERE?
(NAMES OF PLACES)

Where is the hospital?
That is the hospital.
Is that a hospital too?
No, that is not a hospital.
That is the Department of Agriculture.

Where is the Kemang Hotel?

There it is.
Where is the post office?
There it is.
Is that the police station?
Yes, that is right, it is the police station.

Which one is the Town Hall?

That one.
What is this one?
This is a maternity hospital.

PELAJARAN KESEBELAS

DI MANA?
(NAMA TEMPAT)

Di manakah hospital?
Itu hospital.
Itu hospital jugakah?
Bukan, itu bukan hospital.
Itu Jabatan Pertanian.

Di mana Hotel Kemang?

Di situ.
Di mana pejabat pos?
Di sana.
Itukah balai polis?
Ya, betul, itu balai polis.

Yang mana Dewan Orang Ramai?

Yang itu.
Yang ini apa?
Ini hospital bersalin.

THE TWELFTH LESSON

WHICH ONE?

Which one is the hospital?
That one is the hospital.
This one is school.
Which one is the dormitory?
Which one is the post office?
Which one is the briefcase?
This is a briefcase and that one is a writing book.
What is that one?
That one is a typewritter.
What's that?
That is a bird.
Which one is a cat?
That one is a cat.
What is this one?
This one is a dog.

PELAJARAN KEDUA BELAS

YANG MANA?

Yang mana satu hospital?
Yang itu hospital.
Yang ini sekolah.
Yang mana satu asrama?

Yang mana satu pejabat pos?

Yang mana satu beg bimbit?

Yang ini beg bimbit dan yang itu buku tulis.

Yang itu apa?
Yang itu mesin taip.
Itu apa?
Itu burung.
Yang mana kucing?
Yang itu kucing.
Yang ini apa?
Yang ini anjing.

THE THIRTEENTH LESSON

WHERE? (INSTRUMENT)

Where is the knife?	Di mana pisau?
This is a knife.	Ini pisau.
Is there a spoon?	Adakah camca?
Yes, there is.	Ada.
Where is the spoon?	Di mana camca?
Here, Sir.	Di sini, encik.
Here is a spoon.	Ini camca.
What is there?	Di sana apa?
There is a fork.	Di sana garpu.
Where are the dishes?	Piring mana?
Dishes are here.	Piring di sini.
Here are the dishes, spoons and forks.	Di sini ada piring, camca dan garpu.
Glasses too?	Gelas juga?
Glasses too.	Gelas juga.
All of them are here.	Semuanya ada di sini.

THE FOURTEENTH LESSON

STATIONERY, ETC.

Is there any ink?	Adakah dakwat?
Yes, there is.	Ada.

PELAJARAN KETIGA BELAS

DI MANA? (ALATAN)

PELAJARAN KEEMPAT BELAS

ALAT TULIS DAN LAIN-LAIN

Is there a fountain pen?	Adakah pen?
Yes, there is too.	Juga ada.
Where is the dictionary?	Manakah kamus?
Here is the dictionary.	Ini kamus.
Where are the writing books?	Di manakah buku tulis?
Here are the writing books.	Di sini ada buku tulis.
What is this?	Ini apa?
This is a letter and that is an envelope.	Ini surat dan itu sampul surat.
Are there any stamps?	Adakah setem?
Yes, there are stamps.	Ya, ada setem.
Where?	Di mana?
Here in the box.	Dalam kotak.
Rope is here too.	Tali juga ada di sini.

THE FIFTEENTH LESSON

PELAJARAN KELIMA BELAS

POSSESIONS

KEPUNYAAN

This is my book.	Ini buku saya.
This is a textbook.	Ini buku teks.
This is a Bahasa Malaysia textbook.	Ini buku pelajaran Bahasa Malaysia.
That is a book too.	Itu juga buku.
That is a foreign language textbook.	Itu buku teks bahasa asing.
Where is your book?	Mana buku anda?
Here it is.	Di sini.

Here is my book.	Di sini buku saya.
My book is here.	Buku saya di sini.
This is Mr. Green's text-book.	Ini buku pelajaran Encik Green.
This is his book.	Ini bukunya.
Where is Miss Hanako's book?	Di mana buku Cik Hanako?
I don't know.	Saya tidak tahu.
I don't know where her book is.	Saya tidak tahu di mana bukunya berada.

THE SIXTEENTH LESSON

SHOES ETC.

PELAJARAN KEENAM BELAS

KASUT DAN LAIN-LAIN

Where are my shoes?	Mana kasut saya?
Your shoes are there.	Kasut anda di situ.
Mrs. Fokker's shoes are there.	Kasut Puan Fokker ada di situ.
Her shoes are there.	Kasutnya ada di situ.
Men's shoes.	Kasut lelaki.
Ladies' shoes.	Kasut wanita.
Mr. Coa's shoes are men's shoes.	Kasut Encik Coa kasut lelaki.
Mrs. Coa's shoes are ladies' shoes.	Kasut Puan Coa kasut wanita.
Whose shoes are those?	Itu kasut siapa?

Those are Mr. Smith's shoes.

Are Mrs. Smith's shoes men's shoes?

No. Mrs. Smith's shoes are ladies' shoes.

Where are your shoes?

My shoes are here.

Your shoes are in your room.

Itu kasut Encik Smith.

Kasut Puan Smith kasut lelakikah?

Bukan, kasut Puan Smith kasut wanita.

Di mana kasut anda?

Kasut saya di sini.

Kasut anda di bilik anda.

THE SEVENTEENTH LESSON

CIGARETTES & LIGHTER

PELAJARAN KETUJUH BELAS

ROKOK DAN PEMETIK API/MANCIS

Whose cigarettes are thes?

These are Mr. Green's cigarettes.

These are his cigarettes.

This is Miss Hanako's lighter.

This is her lighter.

Where are my cigarettes?

Your cigarettes are over there?

Your lighter is also there.

Ini rokok siapa?

Ini rokok Encik Green.

Ini rokoknya.

Ini pemetik api Cik Hanako.

Ini pemetik apinya.

Di mana rokok saya?

Rokok anda di sana.

Pemetik api anda juga di sana.

16

This is not my cigarette.	Ini bukan rokok saya.
This is not my lighter, either.	Ini juga bukan pemetik api saya.
Do you have a lighter?	Anda ada pemetik api?
No, I don't.	Saya tidak ada.
I don't have a lighter.	Saya tidak ada pemetik api.
I don't have cigarettes.	Saya juga tidak ada rokok.
I don't have cigarettes and a lighter.	Saya tidak ada rokok dan pemetik api.

THE EIGHTEENTH LESSON

ROOMS

PELAJARAN KELAPAN BELAS

BILIK

Where is the sitting room?	Mana bilik tamu?
The sitting room is over there.	Bilik tamu (ada) di situ.
Where is the bedroom?	Di mana bilik tidur?
The bedroom is over there.	Bilik tidur di sana.
Where is the toilet? (little room).	Di mana tandas?
The toilet is here.	Tandas ada di sini.
Is this a toilet?	Tandaskah ini?
It is not a toilet but a bathroom.	Itu bukan tandas, tetapi bilik mandi.

Where is the toilet?	Kalau begitu, tandas di mana?
The toilet is here.	Tandas di sini.
What room is there?	Di situ bilik apa?
There is a bedroom.	Di situ bilik tidur.
There is also a dining room.	Bilik makan juga di situ.
Where are you going?	Encik ke mana?
I'm going to the living room.	Saya pergi ke bilik tamu.

THE NINETEENTH LESSON

DIRECTIONS

PELAJARAN KESEMBILAN BELAS

NAMA ARAH

Where is Mr. Yamada?	Encik Yamada di mana?
He is in the bathroom.	Dia di bilik mandi.
Where is Mr. Fokker?	Encik Fokker di mana?
Mr. Fokker is in the dining room.	Encik Fokker di bilik makan.
Where is Mrs. Sundoro?	Puan Sundoro di mana?
Mrs. Sundoro is in the kitchen.	Puan Sundoro di dapur.
Which one is the kitchen?	Yang mana satu dapur?
That one is the kitchen.	Yang itu dapur.
Where is the garage?	Garaj di mana?
The garage is there.	Garaj di sana.
Is there a car there?	Di situ ada kereta?

Yes, there is.	Ada.
Where is north?	Utara di mana?
North is over there.	Utara di situ.
Then South is there. West is there and East is there.	Kalau begitu Selatan di situ. Barat di sana dan Timur di sana.
The sun rises in the East.	Matahari terbit di Timur.
The sun sets in the West.	Matahari terbenam di Barat.

THE TWENTIETH LESSON	PELAJARAN KEDUA PULUH
THINGS (I)	**BENDA-BENDA (I)**

Here is a bag, an umbrella and walking stick.	Di sini ada beg, payung dan tongkat.
What is there?	Di sana ada apa?
There is a pencil, a fountain pen and ink.	Di sana ada pensil, pen dan dakwat.
Is there any paper?	Adakah kertas?
There is no paper there.	Kertas tidak ada.
What is on the table?	Ada apa di atas meja?
On the table there are a vase and a flower.	Di atas meja ada pasu bunga dan bunga.
What else?	Ada apa lagi?
There is an ashtray.	Ada tempat abuk rokok.
Is there a teapot and a glass?	**Adakah teko dan gelas?**

Yes, there is.	Ya, ada.
What is there in the glass?	Dalam gelas ada apa?
There is some tea.	Ada teh.
There is some coffee in the teapot.	Dalam teko ada kopi.
There is some milk too.	Juga ada susu.

THE TWENTY FIRST LESSON

PELAJARAN KEDUA PULUH SATU

BEDROOM

BILIK TIDUR

What is there in the bedroom?	Di bilik tidur ada apa?
There is a bed in the bedroom.	Di bilik tidur ada katil.
The bed is in the corner.	Katil itu ada di penjuru bilik.
What is there on the bed?	Di atas katil ada apa?
There are matresses, bedsheets, pillows, Dutch wife and blankets.	Ada tilam, cadar, bantal, bantal peluk dan selimut.
There is a lamp too.	Juga ada lampu.
It is an electric lamp.	Ianya lampu elektrik.
What is there under the bed?	Ada apa di bawah katil?
There is nothing.	Tidak ada apa-apa.
There is a desk before the window.	Dekat tingkap ada meja tulis.

There is a chair beside the table.	Di sisi meja ada kerusi.
There is a book on the table.	Di atas meja ada buku.
It is a Bahasa Malaysia textbook.	Itu buku teks Bahasa Malaysia.
There is also a radio, television and a telephone.	Di sini juga ada radio, televisyen dan telefon.
There is a calendar and a painting on the wall.	Di atas dinding ada kalendar dan lukisan.

THE TWENTY SECOND LESSON

THINGS (II)

That's my book.	Itu buku saya.
My book is on the table.	Buku saya ada di atas meja.
Where is your book?	Mana buku encik?
My book is on the chair.	Buku saya ada di atas kerusi.
Where is Mr. Smith's book?	Buku Encik Smith di mana?
Here it is.	Ada di sini.
Where is my briefcase?	Beg bimbit saya di mana?
Your briefcase is on the table.	Beg bimbit anda di atas meja.

PELAJARAN KEDUA PULUH DUA

BENDA-BENDA (II)

21

Where is mother's umbrella?	Payung ibu di mana?
Mother's umbrella is in the bedroom.	Payung ibu di bilik tidur.
Do you have a car.	Anda ada kereta?
Yes, I do. My car is in the garage.	Ya, ada. Kereta saya di garaj.
My car is in the yard.	Kereta saya di halaman.
My bag is in the car.	Beg saya dalam kereta.
My cigarette is in my pocket.	Rokok saya dalam kocek saya.

THE TWENTY-THIRD LESSON

POSSESSION

PELAJARAN KEDUA PULUH TIGA

KEPUNYAAN

Do you have a car?	Anda ada kereta?
Yes, I have a car.	Ya, saya ada kereta.
Mr. Green has a car.	Encik Green ada kereta.
He goes by car.	Dia pergi naik kereta.
I go by scooter.	Saya naik skuter.
Where is your scooter.	Mana skuter anda?
Over there by the road.	Di sana di tepi jalan.
Whose motorcycle is that?	Motosikal siapa itu?
That is Mr. Karim's motorcycle.	Itu motosikal Encik Karim.
Whose house is this?	Ini rumah siapa?

This is Mr Sulaiman's house.	Ini rumah Encik Sulaiman.
Does it have a garage?	Adakah garaj keretanya?
Yes, there is. This house has a garage.	Ya. ada. Rumah ini ada garaj kereta.
There is also TV, radio and telephone.	Televisyen, radio dan telefon pun ada.
They have a typewritter too.	Mereka juga ada mesin taip.

THE TWENTY FOURTH LESSON

AT HOME

PELAJARAN KEDUA PULUH EMPAT

SUASANA DI RUMAH

Where is your television?	Televisyen encik di mana?
Our television is in the living room.	Televisyen kami di ruang tamu.
Where is your telephone?	Telefon encik di mana?
Our telephone is in the bedroom.	Telefon kami di bilik tidur.
Is there a desk in the bedroom?	Adakah meja tulis di bilik tidur?
No, there isn't.	Tidak ada.
The desk is in the study.	Meja tulis di bilik belajar.
Books are in the library.	Buku-buku ada di perpustakaan.
In the study there are also writing materials.	Di bilik belajar ada juga alat-alat tulis.

There are also envelopes and stamps.	Di situ ada juga sampul surat dan setem.
In the kitchen there are cooking utensils.	Di dapur ada alat-alat masak.
In the bathroom is a bucket.	Di bilik mandi ada besen basuh.
There is also a towel and soap.	Di situ juga ada tuala mandi dan sabun.
There are toothbrushes and tooth paste as well.	Berus gigi dan ubat gigi pun ada.
I take a bath in the bathroom.	Saya mandi di bilik mandi.

THE TWENTY FIFTH LESSON

HOTEL, ETC.

PELAJARAN KEDUA PULUH LIMA

HOTEL DAN SEBAGAINYA

Where's Hilton Hotel?	Hotel Hilton di mana?
Hilton Hotel is in Jalan Tun Ismail.	Hotel Hilton di Jalan Tun Ismail.
The Japanese Embassy is in Jalan Tun Abd. Razak.	Kedutaan Besar Jepun di Jalan Tun Abdul Razak.
The American Embassy Building is also there.	Kedutaan Amerika juga di situ.
The Singapore Embassy is also there.	Kedutaan Besar Singapore juga di situ.

Where's Minerva Book Store?

Minerva Book Store is at Jalan Tuanku Abdul Rahman.

Malayan Banking is also at that street.

Across the street from Malayan Banking is Perlis Hotel.

There is President Hotel nearby.

Where's the City Railway Station?

The City Railway Station is in front of the bank.

Where's the post office?

The post office is at the main road.

There are also shops at the main road.

Kedai buku Minerva di mana?

Kedai buku Minerva di Jalan Tuanku Abdul Rahman.

Malayan Banking juga di jalan itu.

Di depan Malayan Banking ialah Hotel Perlis.

Di sebelahnya ada Hotel Presiden.

Di mana stesen keretapi?

Stesen keretapi di depan bank.

Di mana pejabat pos?

Pejabat pos di jalan besar.

Di jalan besar juga ada kedai.

THE TWENTY SIXTH LESSON

YOURS AND HIS

Where is your house?
My house is in Petaling Jaya.
In what part of Petaling Jaya?
At old town.
What part of old town?

On market street.
Mr. Samad's house is in Selayang.
Old or New Selayang?

His house is at New Selayang.
What street in New Selayang?
At number nine.
Is this his house?
Yes, this is his house.
Whose house is over there?
It's Encik Hamid's house over there.

PELAJARAN KEDUA PULUH ENAM

KEPUNYAAN ANDA DAN DIA

Rumah encik di mana?
Rumah saya di Petaling Jaya.
Di Petaling Jaya di mana?

Di kawasan Melayu.
Di kawasan Melayu di mana?
Di Jalan Pasar.
Rumah Encik Samad di Selayang.
Di Selayang Lama atau di Selayang Baru.
Rumahnya di Selayang Baru.
Di jalan apa di Selayang Baru?
Di Jalan Sembilan.
Inikah rumahnya?
Ya, inilah rumahnya.
Yang di sana itu rumah siapa?
Yang di sana itu rumah Encik Hamid.

THE TWENTY SEVENTH LESSON

TOWN HALL ETC

Where is Town Hall.

Town Hall is on Merdeka Selatan Street.
What building is nearby?

The American Embassy is nearby.
Where is the museum?
On Merdeka Barat Street.
There are antiques there.

There is also a library.

Where is R.T.M.?
R.T.M. is also on Merdeka Barat Street.
The Department of Information is also there.
What about the Palace? Where is it?
The Palace is at Jalan Istana.

PELAJARAN KEDUA PULUH TUJUH

DEWAN ORANG RAMAI DAN LAIN-LAIN

Di manakah Dewan Orang Ramai?
Dewan Orang Ramai di Jalan Merdeka Selatan.
Bangunan apakah yang berdekatan?
Bangunan itu ialah Kedutaan Besar Amerika.
Muzium di mana?
Di Jalan Merdeka Barat.
Di situ ada barang-barang antik.
Di situ juga ada perpustakaan.
R.T.M. di mana?
R.T.M. di Jalan Merdeka Barat.
Jabatan Penerangan juga ada di situ.
Di manakah Istana Negara?
Istana Negara di Jalan Istana.

| Where is the City Police Station? | Di manakah Ibu Pejabat Polis? |
| Sorry, I don't know. | Maaf, saya tidak tahu. |

THE TWENTY EIGHTH LESSON

ZOO, ETC

Where is Zoo Negara?	Di manakah Zoo Negara?
Zoo Negara is in Ulu Kelang.	Zoo Negara di Ulu Kelang.
Where is Ulu Kelang?	Ulu Kelang itu di mana?
Ulu Kelang is in Selangor.	Ulu Kelang itu di Selangor.
Where's the secondhand antique shops?	Kedai barang-barang antik di mana?
At Market Street.	di Jalan Pasar.
The bird's market is near Sultan Street.	Kedai burung dekat Jalan Sultan.
The bird's market is a long way (far) from here.	Kedai burung jauh dari sini.
Where is Malaya Hotel?	Hotel Malaya di mana?
It is near Klang Bus Terminal.	Dekat stesen bus Klang.
Near the Lee Rubber Building, isn't it?	Dekat Bangunan Lee Rubber, bukan?
Yes, the hotel is across the street from the Lee Rubber Building.	Ya, hotel itu di seberang jalan dari Bangunan Lee Rubber.

PELAJARAN KEDUA PULUH LAPAN

ZOO DAN LAIN-LAIN

The bus terminal is also across the street from the hotel.	Stesen bus juga ⏤ seberang jalan dengan hotel itu.
Where's the Rex theatre?	Di mana pawagam Rex?
The Rex theatre is in Sultan Street.	Pawagam Rex di Jalan Sultan.

THE TWENTY NINTH LESSON

COUNTING (I)

PELAJARAN KEDUA PULUH SEMBILAN

MENGIRA (I)

Here are manggosteens.	Di sini ada buah manggis.
How many manggosteens teens.	Ada berapa buah manggis di situ?
Please count them:	Cubalah kira:
There are ten manggosteen.	Ada sepuluh buah manggis.
There are ten all together.	Semuanya ada sepuluh buah.
They are ten in all.	Ada sepuluh buah semuanya.
I have ten fingers.	Saya ada sepuluh jari.
I have five fingers on my right hand.	Jari tangan kanan lima.
I have five fingers on my left hand.	Jari tangan kiri juga lima.
I also have ten toes.	Jari kaki juga begitu.
I have ten toes.	Kaki saya ada sepuluh jari.

How many desks are here?	Berapa buah meja tulis di sini?
Only one.	Hanya sebuah.
I have only one cigarette left.	Rokok saya tinggal sebatang sahaja.
Just now there were five.	Tadi masih ada lima batang.

THE THIRTIETH LESSON

COUNTING (II)

How many eggs are there?
There is a basket of them.
Please count:
One, two, three, four, five, six, seven, eight, nine, ten, eleven, twelve, thirteen, fourteen, fifteen, sixteen, seventeen, eighteen, nineteen, twenty, twenty-one.

They are twenty one in all.
Those eggs are twenty-one.

PELAJARAN KETIGA PULUH

MENGIRA (II)

Ada berapa biji telur?
Ada satu bakul.
Cubalah kira:
Satu, dua, tiga, empat, lima, enam, tujuh, lapan, sembilan, sepuluh, sebelas, dua belas, tiga belas, empat belas, lima belas, enam belas, tujuh belas, lapan belas, sembilan belas, dua puluh, dua puluh satu.
Semuanya ada dua puluh satu biji.
Telur ini dua puluh satu biji.

How many eggs are there in one dozen.	Berapa biji dalam sedozen?
There are twelve in a dozen.	Sedozen ada dua belas biji.
I want a dozen eggs.	Saya perlu sedozen telur.
How much is half a dozen.	Kalau setengah dozen berapa?
Half a dozen is six, of course.	Setengah dozen tentu ada enam biji.
I count manggosteen and eggs.	Saya kira, manggis dan telur.
How many are there altogether.	Berapa semuanya?

THE THIRTY-FIRST LESSON

COUNTING (III)

PELAJARAN KETIGA PULUH SATU

MENGIRA (III)

How many tomatoes are there?	Ada berapa biji tomato?
There are four tomatoes.	Ada empat biji.
How many oranges are there?	Ada berapa biji oren?
There are a lot of oranges.	Ada banyak.
How many oranges are there?	Berapa biji oren semuanya?

There are thirty oranges all together.

Semuanya ada tiga puluh biji.

Are there pineapples too?

Nenas juga ada?

Yes, there are one hundred pineapples.

Ya, ada. Nenas ada seratus biji.

There are one thousand dukus.

Duku ada seribu biji.

There are five papayas.

Betik ada lima biji.

Here is a bunch of bananas.

Ini ada pisang satu sisir.

How many bananas does a bunch consist of?

Berapa buah satu sisir?

Please count it.

Cuba kira.

A bunch consists of sixteen bananas.

Satu sisir ada enam belas buah.

I like bananas.

Saya suka pisang.

THE THIRTY SECOND LESSON

PELAJARAN KETIGA PULUH DUA

COUNTING PEOPLE AND ANIMALS

MENGIRA ORANG DAN HAIWAN

Look here!

Lihatlah sini!

There are many children here.

Di sini ada ramai kanak-kanak.

All of them are boys.

Semuanya kanak-kanak lelaki.

There are no girls.

Please count how many people there are?

One, two, three, four, five, six, seven, eight, nine, ten.

There are ten persons all together.

There are seven hens here.

Please count the hens.

One, two, three, four, five, six, seven.

Mrs. Azizah's hens are thirty.

One cock and twenty nine hens.

Then they have many eggs.

Kanak-kanak perempuan tidak ada.

Kiralah berapa orang?

Seorang, dua orang, tiga orang, empat orang, lima orang, enam orang, tujuh orang, lapan orang, sembilan orang, sepuluh orang.

Semuanya ada sepuluh orang.

Di sini ada tujuh ekor ayam.

Kiralah ayam itu.

Seekor, dua ekor, tiga ekor, empat ekor, lima ekor, enam ekor, tujuh ekor.

Ayam Puan Azizah ada tiga puluh ekor.

Seekor ayam jantan dan dua puluh sembilan ayam betina.

Kalau begitu banyak telornya.

THE THIRTY-THIRD LESSON

COUNTING THINGS

Mr. Smith has two pens.

He has three pencil.

Mrs. Hamidah has six pairs of shoes.
He has six clothes.

How many cars do you have?
I have only one car.

Mr. Kassim has one television.
There is a lamp near the television.
Give him a glass of water.
This is a cup of coffee.
And this is a piece of bread.
Mr. Yamada has three books.
This book consists of three volumes.

PELAJARAN KETIGA PULUH TIGA

MENGIRA BENDA

Encik Smith ada dua batang pen.
Dia ada tiga batang pen sel.
Puan Hamidah ada enam pasang kasut.
Dia juga ada enam helai pakaian.
Berapa buah kereta tuan ada?
Saya hanya ada sebuah kereta.
Encik Kasim mempunyai sebuah televisyen.
Dekat televisyen ada sebuah lampu.
Berikan dia segelas air.
Ini ada secawan kopi.
Dan ini ada sekeping roti.

Encik Yamada ada tiga buah buku.
Buku ini ada tiga jilid.

| Volume one, volume two, volume three. | Jilid satu, jilid dua, jilid tiga. |
| This encyclopedia consists of twenty-five volumes. | Eksiklopedia ini ada dua puluh lima jilid. |

| THE THIRTY FOURTH LESSON | PELAJARAN KETIGA PULUH EMPAT |

| **ARITHMETIC** | **KIRA-KIRA** |

How much is two times two?	Dua kali dua berapa?
Two times two is four.	Dua kali dua empat.
How much is two plus two?	Dua tambah dua berapa?
Two plus two is also four?	Dua tambah dua juga empat.
How much is two minus two?	Kalau dua tolak dua berapa?
Two minus two is nil.	Kalau dua tolak dua sifar (kosong).
How much is two divided by two?	Kalau dua dibahagi dua?
Two divided by two is one.	Dua dibahagi dua sama dengan satu.
Two times five is ten.	Dua kali lima sepuluh.
Ten times ten is one hundred.	Sepuluh kali sepuluh seratus.

One hundred minus one is ninety nine.	Seratus tolak satu sama dengan sembilan puluh sembilan.
One thousand plus one is one thousand and one.	Seribu campur satu sama dengan seribu satu.
Three times nine is twenty-seven.	Tiga kali sembilan dua puluh tujuh.
Six times five is thirty.	Enam kali lima tiga puluh.

## THE THIRTY-FIFTH LESSON	## PELAJARAN KETIGA PULUH LIMA
### HOTEL	### HOTEL
My room is on the first floor.	Bilik saya di tingkat pertama.
Miss Hanako's room is on the second floor.	Bilik Cik Hanako di tingkat dua.
Mr. Green's room is on the third floor.	Bilik Encik Green di tingkat tiga.
Mr. Yamada's room is on the fourth floor.	Bilik Encik Yamada di tingkat empat.
I am the fifth person.	Saya orang kelima.
Mr. Sundoro is the sixth guest.	Tuan Sundoro tetamu yang keenam.
Who is the seven quest?	Siapa tetamu yang ketujuh?
Mrs. Fokker is the eighth guest.	Puan Fokker tetamu yang kelapan.

Mr. Affandi is the ninth.	Encik Affandi yang ke-sembilan.
Mr. Smith is the tenth.	Encik Smith orang yang kesepuluh.
Who is the eleventh guest?	Siapa tetamu yang ke-sebelas?
Who lives on the twelfth floor.	Siapa tinggal di tingkat dua belas.
What number is this book?	Ini buku yang ke berapa?
This is the thirteenth book.	Ini buku yang ketigabelas.
This is the fourteenth day I am staying here.	Ini hari yang keempat-belas saya di sini.

THE THIRTY-SIXTH LESSON

FRACTION

How much is one divided by two?	Satu dibahagi dua berapa?
One divided by two is a half.	Satu dibahagi dua sama dengan setengah.
A half means a half part.	Setengah sama dengan separuh.
A half is more than one third.	Setengah lebih banyak daripada satu pertiga.

PELAJARAN KETIGA PULUH ENAM

NOMBOR PECAHAN

37

A fourth is more than one fifth.

One divided by five is one fifth.

One sixth of a dozen is two.

Seven times one seventh is one.

One eight of forty is five.

One ninth is more than a tenth

One eleventh is more than a twelfth.

Two and three fourths.

One thirteenth is more than one fourteenth.

One fifteenth is more than one sixteenth.

seperempat lebih banyak daripada satu perlima.

Satu dibahagi lima sama dengan satu perlima.

Satu perenam daripada sedozen sama dengan dua.

Tujuh kali satu pertujuh sama dengan satu.

Satu perlapan daripada empat puluh sama dengan lima.

Satu persembilan lebih daripada satu persepuluh.

Satu persebelas lebih daripada satu perdua belas.

Dua tiga perempat.

Satu pertiga belas lebih daripada satu perempat belas.

Satu perlima belas lebih daripada satu perenam belas.

THE THIRTY-SEVENTH LESSON

JOBS (I)

Let me introduce Mr. William (to you).

What's Mr William's job?

Mr. William is a merchant.

Is Mrs. William a merchant?
No, Mrs. William is not a merchant.

Mrs. William is a teacher.

Where does she teach?
She teaches at Kolej Tuanku Abdul Rahman.
Who is that man?
He is Mr. Smith, an American Embassy official.
What about Mrs. Smith?
Mrs. Smith doesn't work. She just stays home.

PELAJARAN KETIGA PULUH TUJUH

PEKERJAAN (I)

Biar saya perkenalkan anda dengan Encik William.

Apakah pekerjaan Encik William?

Encik William ialah seorang ahli perniagaan.

Puan William pun ahli perniagaankah?
Tidak, Puan William bukan seorang ahli perniagaan.

Puan William ialah seorang guru.

Dia mengajar di mana?
Dia mengajar di Kolej Tuanku Abdul Rahman.
Siapa lelaki itu?
Encik Smith, pegawai kedutaan besar Amerika.

Puan Smith bagaimana?
Puan Smith tidak bekerja.
Dia hanya seorang surirumah sahaja.

What is Mr. Chong's job?	Apakah pekerjaan Encik Chong?
I don't know.	Saya tidak tahu.

THE THIRTY-EIGHT LESSON

JOBS (II)

PELAJARAN KETIGA PULUH LAPAN

PEKERJAAN (II)

How many persons are there?	Berapa orang di sana?
Let me count them first.	Cuba saya kira dulu.
There are five persons all together.	Ada lima orang semuanya.
Who are those people?	Siapakah orang-orang itu?
They are a teacher, a policeman and three children.	Seorang guru, seorang polis dan tiga orang kanak-kanak.
How many employees are there?	Berapa orang pekerja di sini?
There are forty employees here.	Di sini ada empat puluh orang pekerja.
Quite a number, aren't they?	Banyak juga, ya?
There are two typists.	Ada dua orang jurutaip.
How many clerks are there?	Ada berapa orang kerani?
He used to be a pilot.	Dulu dia seorang juru-terbang.

He used to be a merchant.
Now he is a cook.

That taxi driver used to be a seaman.
His father is a farmer.

Dia pernah jadi saudagar.
Kini dia jadi tukang masak.

Pemandu teksi itu dulu seorang pelaut.
Ayahnya seorang petani.

THE THIRTY-NINTH LESSON

MONEY (I)

What money is this?
This is Malaysian money.
This is a banknote.
This is a one hundred ringgit bill.
This is a five hundred ringgit bill.
This is a one thousand ringgit bill.
Where is the five thousand ringgit bill?
This one is a ten thousand ringgit bill.
We also have coins.

This is a one ringgit coin.

PELAJARAN KETIGA PULUH SEMBILAN

WANG (I)

Ini wang apa?
Ini wang Malaysia.
Wang ini wang kertas.
Ini wang kertas seratus ringgit.
Ini wang kertas lima ratus ringgit.
Ini wang kertas seribu ringgit.
Mana wang kertas lima ribu ringgit?
Yang ini wang kertas sepuluh ribu ringgit.
Kami juga ada wang syiling dua puluh sen.
Ini wang syiling satu ringgit.

This is a five ringgit coin.

And this is a twenty five ringgit coin.

We also have ten ringgit coins.

This one is a fifty cent coin.

We also have a twenty cent coin.

Ini wang syiling lima ringgit.

Dan ini wang syiling dua puluh lima ringgit.

Kami juga ada wang syiling sepuluh ringgit.

Yang ini wang syiling lima puluh sen.

Kami juga ada wang syiling dua puluh sen.

THE FORTIETH LESSON

PELAJARAN KEEMPAT PULUH

PRICES (I)

HARGA (I)

How much is that pineapple?

Berapa harga nanas itu?

One dollar and fifty cents.

Seringgit lima puluh sen.

That is expensive.

Itu mahal.

No, Madam, this is not expensive.

Tidak, puan, ini tidak mahal.

May I make a bargain?

Bolehkah saya tawar?

Yes, of course.

Tentu boleh.

May I take it for seventy five cents?

Tujuh puluh lima sen bagaimana?

No, Madam.

Tidak boleh, puan.

What is the fixed price?

Berapa harga pastinya?

One ringgit, madam.

Seringgit, puan.

Can't I get less?

That is already reasonable, Madam.

How many do you want?

One is enough.

Here is the money.

Tak boleh kurang lagi?

Itu sudah patut, puan.

Berapa buah puan mahu?

Cukup sebuah saja.

Ini wangnya.

THE FORTY-FIRST LESSON

PELAJARAN KEEMPAT PULUH SATU

PRICES (II)

HARGA (II)

How much is this paper per sheet?

Berapakah kertas ini sehelai?

Which one, Sir?

Yang mana, encik?

The white and the red one.

Yang putih dan yang merah itu.

This paper is for making flags.

Kertas ini untuk membuat bendera.

It costs 30 cents, a sheet, Sir.

Harga sehelai tiga puluh sen, encik.

Just twenty five cents.

Dua puluh lima sen sajalah.

Can I get less?

Boleh kurangkah?

No, Sir.

Tidak boleh, encik.

That is the fixed price.

Itu harga pasti.

Give me one hundred white sheets and one hundred red sheets.

Beri seratus helai yang merah dan seratus helai yang putih.

How much is it all together?	Berapa semua?
Six dollars.	Semuanya enam ringgit.
Here is a ten ringgit bill.	Ini wangnya sepuluh ringgit.
Here is four ringgit change.	Ini bakinya empat ringgit.
Thank you, Sir.	Terima kasih, encik.
Not at all.	Sama-sama.

THE FORTY-SECOND LESSON

MONEY (II)

PELAJARAN KEEMPAT PULUH DUA

WANG (II)

How much is this pen?	Pen ini berapa harganya?
Two ringgit, Sir.	Dua ringgit, encik.
Can't I get it less?	Tidak boleh kurang?
Yes, you may bargain it.	Ya, boleh ditawar, encik.
I want a writing book.	Saya hendak buku tulis.
The thin one or the thick one?	Yang nipis atau yang tebal?
The rather thicker one.	Yang agak tebal.
Here you are, Sir.	Ini, encik.
This is a thick writing book.	Ini buku tulis tebal.
How much is it?	Berapa sebuah?
Just one ringgit.	Cuma seringgit, encik.

This is a five ringgit bill.

Here is four ringgit change.

Thank you, Sir.
You are welcome.

Ini wang kertas lima ringgit.

Ini wang kembali empat ringgit.

Terima kasih, encik.
Sama-sama.

THE FORTY-THIRD LESSON

DRINK, BEVERAGES

Do you like whiskey?
No, I don't.
Whiskey is too strong.
I just take beer.
I like to drink coffee.
Kim Leng is a big store.

This store opens from nine in the morning to ten at night.
This is a department store.
There are food and drinks in the basement.
Where is the clothing department?

PELAJARAN KEEMPAT PULUH TIGA

MINUMAN

Encik suka wiski?
Tidak, saya tidak suka.
Wiski terlalu keras.
Saya minum bir sahaja.
Saya suka minum kopi.
Kedai Kim Leng adalah sebuah kedai yang besar.
Kedai ini dibuka dari jam sembilan pagi hingga sepuluh malam.
Kedai ini adalah kedai serbaneka.
Di bahagian bawah ada makanan dan minuman.
Di mana bahagian pakaian?

In this department there are all kinds of food.

Di bahagian ini ada bermacam-macam jenis makanan.

There is bread, butter, cheese, cakes and candies.

Ada roti, mentega, keju, kuih-muih dan gula-gula.

There is coffee, milk, tea, beer, whiskey and wine.

Ada kopi, susu, teh, bir, wiski dan wain.

There is meat, eggs and fish.

Ada daging, telur dan ikan.

THE FORTY-FOURTH LESSON

PELAJARAN KEEMPAT PULUH EMPAT

PRICES OF FOOD (I)

HARGA MAKANAN (I)

What meat is this?
Ini daging apa?

This is beef.
Ini daging lembu.

Do you have mutton here?
Adakah daging kambing di sini?

Yes, I do.
Ya, ada.

We have beef, mutton and others.
Di sini ada daging lembu, daging kambing dan lain-lain.

We also have rabbit meat.
Juga ada daging arnab.

Where is your price list?
Mana senarai harga?

Here it is, Sir.
Ini, encik.

How much is the bread?
Roti itu berapa harganya?

It is fifty cent.
Harganya lima puluh sen.

Can I get it less?	Boleh kurang?
No, Madam.	Tidak boleh, puan.
It's fixed price.	Itu harga pasti.
How much is butter per can?	Berapa harga satu tin mentega?
Dua ringgit and sixty cent.	Dua ringgit enam puluh sen.

THE FORTY-FIFTH LESSON

PELAJARAN KEEMPAT PULUH LIMA

PRICES OF FOOD (II)

HARGA MAKANAN (II)

How much is sugar per kilogram?	Gula itu berapa sekilo?
Sugar is one ringgit and thirty sen per kilogram.	Gula sekilo seringgit tiga puluh sen.
How much is coffee per kilogram?	Kopi berapa sekilo?
This is genuine coffee.	Kopi ini kopi tulen.
This is genuine coffee.	Kopi ini kopi asli.
How much is the tea per package?	Teh satu bungkus berapa?
Tea per package is two ringgit.	Teh satu bungkus dua ringgit.
Please give me ¼ kg coffee, 2 kilograms sugar, 3 packages of tea, and 5 bottles of oranges.	Beri saya ¼ kg kopi, gula 2 kg, teh 3 bungkus dan oren 5 botol.

Okay, Sir.
How much does an egg cost?

One egg costs 18 cent.

How much does a fish cost?
The big one costs four ringgit.
The small one costs less.

What's the fixed price?

Baik, encik.
Telur sebiji berapa?

Telur sebiji lapan belas sen, encik.
Ikan seekor berapa?

Yang besar itu empat ringgit, seekor.
Yang kecil harganya kurang.
Berapa harga pasti?

THE FORTY SIXTH LESSON

PICKPOCKETS

Beware of pickpokets!
His money has been stolen.
His watch has been snatched.
Thief! Thief!
Please take care of your money.
Call the police!
The pickpoket is black and blue.

PELAJARAN KEEMPAT PULUH ENAM

PENYELUK SAKU

Awas penyeluk saku!
Wangnya dicuri orang kelmarin.
Jam tangannya kena rentap kelmarin.
Pencuri! Pencuri!
Hati-hati wang anda.

Panggil polis.
Penyeluk poket itu lebam-lebam.

He has been hit by the crowd. | Dia dipukul oleh orang ramai.

Fortunately, the police came quickly. | Untunglah polis cepat sampai.

The police caught the thief immediately. | Polis segera menangkap pencuri itu.

He has been taken to the nearest police station. | Dia dibawa ke balai polis yang terdekat.

He was arrested there for the time being. | Dia telah ditahan di situ buat sekarang.

May be he will be imprisoned. | Barangkali dia akan dipenjarakan.

It was a great pity. | Sungguh kasihan.

The poor thief. | Pencuri yang malang.

THE FORTY-SEVENTH LESSON

PELAJARAN KEEMPAT PULUH TUJUH

DEPARTMENT STORE (I)

KEDAI SERBANIKA (I)

There is furniture in Sarinah's store. | Di kedai Sarinah ada perkakas rumah.

There are also musical instruments. | Ada juga alat-alat muzik.

Are there children's toys too. | Adakah juga mainan kanak-kanak?

Yes, of course. | Ya, tentu ada.

They sell tables and chairs there.

Di sana ada dijual kerusi dan meja.

They also sell cupboards and beds.

Juga ada dijual almari dan katil.

There are musical instruments such as violin and guitars.

Di sana ada alat-alat muzik seperti biola dan gitar.

They also sell flutes and trumpets.

Juga dijual seruling dan terompet.

There are also drums and piano.

Juga dijual dram dan piano.

There are many toys for children.

Mainan kanak-kanak banyak sekali.

Toy cars, dolls, toy guns, etc.

Ada kereta mainan, anak patung mainan, pistol mainan dan lain-lain.

There are also toy trains and toy planes.

Juga terdapat keretapi mainan dan kapal terbang mainan.

There are even toy tanks.

Bahkan ada juga tank mainan.

Toy ships are numerous.

Kapal-kapal mainan juga banyak.

Everything is available. It is up to you to pick out.

Semuanya ada. Terpulang kepada anda untuk memilih.

THE FORTY-EIGHTH LESSON

DEPARTMENT STORE (II)

There are all kinds of clothes in that store.

There are trousers, shirts, skirts and pyjamas.

There are ladies dresses and gent's clothes.

There are also children's clothes.

They consist of different colours.

There are red, green, blue black and brown clothes.

There are dark blue, light blue, dark red, and light red clothes.

Some are also grey and dark brown.

There are also purple clothes.

I like white shirts.

Unfortunately they get dirty easily.

How much is this shirt per piece.

PELAJARAN KEEMPAT PULUH LAPAN

KEDAI SERBANIKA (II)

Di kedai itu juga ada bermacam-macam pakaian.

Ada seluar, kemeja, skirt, dan baju tidur.

Ada pakaian wanita dan juga pakaian lelaki.

Pakaian kanak-kanak pun ada.

Ada bermacam-macam warnanya.

Ada pakaian merah, hijau, biru, hitam dan coklat.

Ada biru tua, biru muda, merah tua dan merah muda.

Ada juga yang berwarna kelabu dan coklat tua.

Yang berwarna ungu juga ada.

Saya suka kemeja putih.

Malangnya ia lekas kotor.

Berapa kemeja ini sehelai?

THE FORTY-NINTH LESSON

SIZE OF CLOTHES

How much is this shirt?

This is a very beautiful shirt.
This a new fashionable shirt.
What size is it?
Large, medium or small sizes?
How much is this long sleeve shirts?
Twenty five ringgit and ninety cents.
Prices are soaring nowadays.
Who is this shirt for?
This shirt is for me.
There is also the cheap one.
There is also the dear one.
I would rather have the most expensive one.
As for me the cheaper one will do.

PELAJARAN KEEMPAT PULUH SEMBILAN

UKURAN PAKAIAN

Kemeja ini berapa harganya?
Kemeja ini cantik sekali.

Kemeja ini fesyen baru.

Berapa saiznya?
Saiz besar, sedang atau kecil?
Berapa harga kemeja lengan panjang ini?
Dua puluh lima ringgit sembilan puluh sen.
Sekarang harga sedang melambung tinggi.
Kemeja ini untuk siapa?
Kemeja ini untuk saya.
Yang murah juga ada.

Yang lebih mahal juga ada.
Saya lebih suka yang mahal sekali.
Kalau saya biar yang lebih murah.

| I do not have enough money. | Wang saya tak cukup. |

<table>
<tr><td>

THE FIFTIETH LESSON

</td><td>

PELAJARAN KELIMA PULUH

</td></tr>
<tr><td>

BARGAINING

</td><td>

TAWAR MENAWAR

</td></tr>
</table>

You can get it less.	Harga ini boleh dikurangkan.
You can get 10 per cent discount.	Sepuluh peratus diskaun boleh diperolehi.
The trousers department is over there.	Di sana tempat penjualan seluar.
Some are long and some are short.	Ada yang panjang dan ada yang pendek.
Some are thick and some are thin.	Ada yang tebal dan ada yang nipis.
There are also different kinds of clothing materials.	Terdapat juga bermacam-macam pakaian
Some are made of cotton and some are made of wool.	Ada yang diperbuat daripada kapas, dan ada yang diperbuat daripada bulu.
Some are made of nylon and some are made of silk.	Ada yang diperbuat daripada nilon dan sutera.
They have different prices.	Harganya juga bermacam-macam.

Some are expensive and some are inexpensive.
The expensive one is $50.00.
The inexpensive one is $30.00.
Is that woollen tie or a nylon tie?
That is a woollen tie.

Ada yang mahal dan ada yang murah.
Yang mahal $50.00.

Yang murah $30.00.

Itu tali leher daripada bulu atau daripada nilon?
Itu tali leher daripada bulu.

FIFTY-FIRST LESSON

SHOPPING (I)

Where are you going?
I am going for shopping.

Where are you going for shopping?
To Ampang Park or to Jalan Tuanku Abdul Rahman.
What will you buy?

All kinds of things.
Everything is very expensive nowadays.

PELAJARAN KELIMA PULUH SATU

MEMBELI-BELAH (I)

Anda hendak ke mana?
Saya hendak ke kedai untuk membeli-belah.
Ke mana anda akan membeli-belah?
Ke Ampang Park atau ke Jalan Tuanku Abdul Rahman.
Apa yang hendak anda beli?
Macam-macam barang.
Barang-barang mahal se-karang

Yes, everything is expensive.	Ya, barang-barang memang mahal harganya.
Where are you shopping?	Di manakah anda akan membeli-belah?
I am shopping just at Ampang Park.	Saya akan ke Ampang Park sahaja.
There is a clothing store there.	Di sana ada kedai pakaian.
There are all kinds of clothes here.	Di sana juga ada bermacam-macam pakaian.
There are shirts, trousers and handkerchiefs.	Ada kemeja, seluar dan saputangan.
There are underwears and hats.	Pakaian dalam dan topi pun ada dijual.
There are gloves, shoes and bags.	Ada sarung tangan, kasut dan beg tangan.

FIFTY SECOND LESSON

PELAJARAN KELIMA PULUH DUA

SHOPPING (II)

MEMBELI-BELAH (II)

There are socks sold over there.	Di sana ada dijual stokin.
Some are stockings and some are socks.	Ada stokin panjang dan pendek.
There are also ties and scarfs.	Juga ada tali leher dan skaf.
I want to buy a towel.	Saya hendak membeli tuala mandi.

I want to buy a jacket and a skirt.	Saya hendak membeli jaket dan skirt.
Do you also have ladies' shoes?	Adakah juga kasut wanita?
Yes, of course.	Tentu ada.
This is a departmental store	Ini kedai serbanika.
Everything is available here/Everything can be bought here.	Apa saja boleh didapati di sini./Segala-galanya boleh dibeli di sini.
I want to buy T-shirts.	Saya hendak membeli baju-T.
I want to buy singlets too.	Saya juga hendak membeli singlet.
Sweater are also available here.	Di sini juga ada dijual baju panas.
I want to buy hand-kerchieves.	Saya hendak membeli saputangan.
I always lose my hand-kerchief.	Sapu tangan saya selalu hilang.
So do I.	Saya juga begitu.

FIFTY THIRD LESSON

SHOPPING (III)

How much are these shoes?

PELAJARAN KELIMA PULUH TIGA

MEMBELI-BELAH (III)

Berapa harga kasut ini sepasang?

Forty ringgit, Sir.	Empat puluh ringgit, encik.
What about this one?	Kalau yang ini?
This one is fifty five ringgit.	Yang ini lima puluh lima ringgit.
Can I get it for forty five dollars?	Empat puluh lima ringgit saja bolehkah?
No, Sir.	Tak boleh, encik.
For whom is that skirt?	Skirt itu untuk siapa?
For my wife.	Untuk isteri saya.
The skirt does not fade.	Skirt itu tidak luntur.
The skirt is endurable.	Skirt itu tahan lama.
I want to buy under-garment.	Saya hendak membeli pakaian dalam.
My undergarment has worn-out.	Pakaian dalam saya sudah koyak.
Anything else, Sir?	Apa lagi, encik?
That's all.	Hanya itu saja.
Next time I'll come here for shopping.	Lain kali saya akan mem-beli-belah di sini lagi.

FIFTY-FOURTH LESSON

PELAJARAN KELIMA PULUH EMPAT

SHOPPING (IV)

MEMBELI-BELAH (IV)

I want to buy a washing soap.	Saya hendak membeli sabun basuh.
Bathing soap too.	Sabun mandi juga.

Here we also have tooth-brushes.	Di sini juga ada dijual berus gigi.
Please give me a tooth-paste.	Berikan saya ubat gigi.
What about combs?	Sikat?
Combs too (I need combs too).	Sikat juga.
Can you send them home?	Bolehkah anda hantar ke rumah?
Yes, of course. What is your address?	Boleh. Alamat encik di mana?
Number 9, Jalan Bunga, Selayang Baru.	Nombor 9, Jalan Bunga, Selayang Baru.
Where is the bread store?	Di mana kedai roti?
I want to buy some bread and butter.	Saya hendak membeli roti dan mentega.
I want to buy slippers too.	Saya juga hendak membeli selipar.
I want to buy a lot of things.	Banyak barang yang hendak saya beli.
I want to buy vegetables and fruits.	Saya juga hendak membeli sayur dan buah-buahan.
Gosh, you have bought a lot of things.	Wah, banyak sekali puan berbelanja.

FIFTY FIFTH LESSON

WEATHER (I)

Gosh, it's fine today!
Yes, it's quite fine.
The sky is clear.
The sun is shining brightly.
Yesterday it was bad.
The sky was cloudy.
The wind blew hard.
The day before yesterday it was just the same.
It rained heavily.
The river overflowed.
The streets were flooded.
There was flood everywhere.
Many cars had engine trouble.
Many trees fell down.

Electric wires were cut off.

PELAJARAN KELIMA PULUH LIMA

CUACA (I)

Wah, hari ini cuaca baik.
Ya, bagus sekali.
Langit cerah.
Matahari bersinar terang.

Kelmarin cuaca buruk.
Langit mendung.
Angin bertiup kencang.
Kelmarin dulu cuaca sama saja.
Hujan lebat.
Sungai menjadi banjir.
Jalan-jalan dipenuhi air.
Banjir di merata-rata tempat.
Banyak kereta yang tersadai (rosak).
Pokok-pokok banyak yang tumbang.
Dawai-dawai elektrik terputus.

FIFTY-SIXTH LESSON

WEATHER (II)

What about tomorrow?
Tomorrow it may be fine.

I hope so.
What about the day after tomorrow?
Will the day after tomorrow be fine?
I guess (think) it will be fine.
What about the three more days?
Let's see the weather forecast.
It will drizzle.

So we would need an umbrella.
I always take an umbrella with me.
I don't want to get wet.
I don't want to be caught in the rain.
I don't want to catch a cold.

PELAJARAN KELIMA PULUH ENAM

CUACA (II)

Bagaimana besok?
Besok cuaca mungkin baik.
Saya harap begitu.
Lusa bagaimana?

Adakah lusa cuaca akan baik?
Saya fikir cuaca akan baik.
Tiga hari lagi bagaimana?

Mari kita lihat ramalan cuaca.
Hari akan hujan renyai-renyai.
Kalau begitu kita perlukan payung.
Saya selalu membawa payung.
Saya takut basah.
Saya tidak mahu terperangkap dalam hujan.
Saya takut kena selsema

You better take a raincoat with you.	**Baik anda bawa baju hujan bersama.**

FIFTY-SEVENTH LESSON

PELAJARAN KELIMA PULUH TUJUH

WEATHER (III)

CUACA (III)

Now it is very hot.	**Sekarang hari panas sekali.**
Yesterday it was hot, too.	**Kelmarin juga panas.**
Last night was also hot.	**Malam semalam juga panas.**
It is always hot.	**Hari selalu panas.**
Everyday it is awfully hot.	**Tiap-tiap hari panas terik.**
Kuala Lumpur is hot.	**Kuala Lumpur panas.**
Kuala Lumpur is extremely hot.	**Kuala Lumpur panas sekali.**
Bukit Fraser is cool.	**Bukit Fraser sejuk.**
Cameron Highlands is cooler.	**Cameron Highlands lebih sejuk.**
Penang Hill is also cool.	**Bukit Bendera juga sejuk.**
The seashore is also cool.	**Tepi pantai juga sejuk.**
I like a cool town.	**Saya suka bandar yang sejuk.**
I can't bear the heat.	**Saya tak tahan panas.**
As for me it is otherwise.	**Bagi saya adalah sebaliknya.**
I can't bear cold.	**Saya tak tahan sejuk.**

WEATHER (IV)

CUACA (IV)

Today it is cloudy.	Sekarang hari mendung.
The sky is covered by the clouds.	Langit dilitupi awan.
There is a great deal of black clouds.	Banyak sekali awan hitam.
The sun cannot be seen.	Matahari tak kelihatan.
It is awfully hot.	Hari panas sekali.
The sun is covered by the cloud.	Matahari dilitupi awan.
Maybe it will rain.	Mungkin hari akan hujan.
There is the sound of thunder.	Ada bunyi guruh.
The wind begins to blow.	Angin mulai bertiup.
The rain begins to fall.	Hujan mulai turun.
It is getting cold.	Hari menjadi sejuk.
My, it is freezing.	Aduh, sejuk sekali.
It is extremely cold.	Sejuk sampai ke tulang sumsum.
I am trembling with chil.	Saya menggigil kesejukan.
I may catch a cold.	Saya mungkin dapat selsema.

WEATHER (V)

(CUACA IV)

Yesterday it was fine.	Kelmarin cuaca baik.
The sky was clear.	Langit cerah.
The sky was completely cloudless.	Langit tak berawan sama sekali.
The sun was shining brightly.	Matahari bersinar terang.
It was a clear night.	Malam hari juga langit cerah.
The moon was shining.	Bulan bersinar.
It was full moon.	Bulan purnama.
The stars are scattered all over the sky.	Bintang-bintang bertaburan di langit.
Many people were seen taking a stroll.	Ramai orang kelihatan bersiar-siar.
They were sitting in the park.	Mereka duduk-duduk di taman.
Children were playing outside.	Kanak-kanak bermain-main di luar.
People preferred to go outdoors.	Orang lebih suka keluar rumah.
The wind was blowing softly.	Angin berhembus sepoi-sepoi bahasa.
The air was cool.	Udara sejuk.
Everyone were happy.	Semua orang gembira.

SIXTIETH LESSON

DATES (I)

What date is today?
Look at the calendar.
Today is Sunday.
Tomorrow is Monday.
The day after tomorrow is Tuesday.
Yesterday was Saturday.
The day before yesterday was Friday.
What day was it 3 days ago?
It was Thursday.
What day is after Thursday?
After Thursday is Friday.

What day is before Thursday?
Before Thursday is Wednesday.
How many days are there in a week?
There are seven days in a week.

PELAJARAN KEENAM PULUH

HARIBULAN (I)

Berapa haribulan hari ini?
Lihatlah kalendar.
Hari ini hari Ahad.
Besok hari Isnin.
Lusa hari Selasa.

Kelmarin hari Sabtu.
Kelmarin dulu hari Jumaat.
Tiga hari yang lalu hari apa?
Hari Khamis.
Selepas hari Khamis hari apa?
Selepas hari Khamis hari Jumaat.
Sebelum hari Khamis hari apa?
Sebelum hari Khamis hari Rabu.
Seminggu ada berapa hari?
Seminggu ada tujuh hari.

VACATION, HOLIDAY

HARI CUTI

When is our holiday?
Sunday.
What day does the office
  close at 12.00?
Friday.
Why 12.00 o'clock?
The Muslims go to the
  Mosque on that day.
What time does the office
  close on Saturdays?
On Saturday the office
  closes at one o'clock.
How many days will you
  be in Singapore?
I'll stay in Singapore for
  3 days.
I'll stay there for 3 days.

When will you go to
  Sabah?
May be on Tuesday.
Next Tuesday.
We'll on leave from Tues-
  day onwards.

Hari apa cuti kita?
Hari Ahad.
Hari apa pejabat tutup
  jam 12.00 tengahari?
Hari Jumaat.
Mengapa pukul 12.00?
Kaum muslimin pergi ke
  masjid.
Pukul berapa pejabat
  tutup hari Sabtu?
Hari Sabtu pejabat tutup
  pukul satu.
Berapa hari anda akan
  berada di Singapura?
Saya akan tinggal di
  Singapura 3 hari.
Saya akan tinggal di sana
  3 hari.
Hari apa anda akan pergi
  ke Sabah?
Barangkali hari Selasa.
Hari Selasa depan.
Hari Selasa, kami akan
  mulai cuti.

SIXTY-SECOND LESSON

MONTHS OF THE YEAR

What month is this?

This is January.

What month is next month?

Next month is February.

What month comes after February?

March.

What month was last month?

Last month was December?

What month comes before December?

November.

How many months are there in a year?

There are twelve months in a year.

January, February, March, April.

May, June, July, August, September.

PELAJARAN KEENAM PULUH DUA

BULAN

Bulan ini bulan apa?

Bulan Januari.

Bulan depan bulan apa?

Bulan depan bulan Februari.

Selepas Februari bulan apa?

Bulan Mac.

Bulan yang lalu bulan apa?

Bulan yang lalu bulan Disember.

Sebelum Disember bulan apa?

Bulan November.

Ada berapa bulan dalam setahun?

Setahun ada dua belas bulan.

Januari, Februari, Mac, April.

Mei, Jun, Julai, Ogos, September.

October, November and December.

Oktober, November dan Disember.

SIXTY-THIRD LESSON

SEASONS

When is winter in Europe?

Winter is in December, January and February.

When is rainy season?
Rainy season is in October, November, December, January, February, and March.
When is the dry season?

Dry season is in April until September.
How many days are there in a month?
There are 30 or 31 days in a month.
There are 28 days and sometimes 29 days in February.

PELAJARAN KEENAM PULUH TIGA

MUSIM

Bulan apa musim sejuk di Eropah?
Musim sejuk bulan Disember, Januari dan Februari.
Bulan apa musim hujan?
Musim hujan bulan Oktober, November, Disember, Januari, Februari dan Mac.
Bulan apa musim kemarau?
Musim kemarau bulan April hingga September.
Berapa hari dalam sebulan?
Sebulan ada 30 hari atau 31 hari.
Bulan Februari kadang-kadang 28 hari dan kadang-kadang 29 hari.

In Malaysia there are two kinds of months.

They are solar and lunar months
(Christian and Hegira months).

Di Malaysia ada dua jenis bulan.

Bulan Masehi dan bulan Hijrah.

SIXTY-FOURTH LESSON

PELAJARAN KEENAM PULUH EMPAT

DATES (II)

HARIBULAN (II)

What date is today?

Today is the 5th of January.

What date is tomorrow?

Tomorrow is the 6th of January.

What date is the day after tomorrow?

The day after tomorrow is the sixth (of January).

What date was yesterday?

Yesterday was the fourth.

When does he get his salary?

Haribulan berapa hari ini?

Hari ini 5 haribulan Januari.

Besok berapa haribulan?

Besok 6 haribulan Januari.

Lusa berapa haribulan?

Lusa tujuh haribulan.

Kelmarin berapa haribulan?

Kelmarin empat haribulan.

Berapa haribulan dia terima gaji?

68

On the thirtieth of every month.	30 haribulan tiap-tiap bulan.
When is the New Year?	Bilakah tahun baru?
The New Year is on the first of January.	Tahun baru pada 1 haribulan Januari.
When is Chrismas?	Bilakah hari Natal?
Christmas is on 25th of December.	Hari Natal pada 25 haribulan Disember.

SIXTY-FIFTH LESSON	PELAJARAN KEENAM PULUH LIMA
DATES (III)	HARIBULAN (III)

Is 25th December is a holiday?	Adakah 25 Disember hari cuti umum?
Yes, it is.	Ya, hari cuti.
Did you receive my Christmas card?	Adakah tuan terima kad hari Natal saya?
Yes, I did. Thank you.	Ya, ada, terima kasih.
When are you leaving?	Bilakah tuan akan berangkat?
I am leaving on the tenth.	Saya akan berangkat pada sepuluh haribulan.
When will you come back?	Bilakah tuan akan kembali?
I will come back on the fifteenth.	Saya akan kembali pada lima belas haribulan.

On the twentieth I'll be off again.

Pada dua puluh haribulan saya berangkat lagi.

Where will you go on the twentieth?

Ke mana tuan pergi pada dua puluh haribulan?

I will go to Medan.

Saya akan ke Medan.

When will you be back to Kuala Lumpur?

Bilakah tuan akan kembali ke Kuala Lumpur?

May be on the twenty fifth.

Mungkin pada dua puluh lima haribulan.

When shall we go on a picnic?

Bilakah kita akan pergi berkelah?

We shall go on the ninth of march.

Kita akan pergi pada sembilan Mac.

SIXTY-SIXTH LESSON

PELAJARAN KEENAM PULUH ENAM

INDEPENDENCE DAY

HARI KEMERDEKAAN

What date is the Malaysia's Independence Day?

Bilakah Hari Kemerdekaan Malaysia?

The thirty first of August.

Malaysia merdeka pada 31hb Ogos.

What year was it?

Tahun berapa?

The year nineteen fifty seven.

Tahun Seribu Sembilan Ratus Lima Puluh Tujuh

It was the Independence Day for Malaysia.

Every thirty first of August is a holiday.

On that day Independence Day is celebrated.

There is a flag-hoisting ceremony.

The ceremony is sometimes held at the Merdeka Stadium.

So are the parades and processions.

At night there will be a variety show.

Hari itu adalah hari Kemerdekaan Tanah Melayu (Malaysia).

Tiap tiga puluh satu Ogos cuti am.

Hari itu diadakan upacara hari kemerdekaan.

Ada upacara menaikkan bendera Malaysia.

Upacara itu kadang-kadang diadakan di Stadium Merdeka.

Juga diadakan perbarisan.

Di sebelah malam diadakan pertunjukan aneka ragam.

SIXTY-SEVENTH LESSON

PELAJARAN KEENAM PULUH TUJUH

BIRTHDAY

HARI JADI

When were you born?
I was born on October the fifth.
It is the armed forces Day.

Bilakah anda dilahirkan?
Saya dilahirkan pada lima Oktober.
Ianya hari Angkatan Bersenjata.

Mr. Smith's birthday is on the 10th of December.	Hari lahir Encik Smith ialah pada 10 Disember.
Where were you born?	Di mana encik dilahirkan?
I was born in Tokyo.	Saya dilahirkan di Tokyo.
That mother gave birth to a baby boy.	Ibu itu melahirkan bayi lelaki.
The baby is crying very loudly.	Bayi itu menangis kuat sekali.
When did you receive the letter?	Bilakah encik terima surat itu?
I received the letter on the eight of this month.	Surat itu saya terima pada lapan haribulan.
What date will next Monday be?	Hari Isnin yang akan datang berapa haribulan?
The 28th of November.	28 November.
When did you move here?	Bilakah encik pindah ke sini?
On last 27th.	Pada 27 haribulan yang lalu.
I have been here just five days.	Saya baru lima hari di sini.

ITINERARY

When did you arrive in
Kuala Lumpur?
I arrived three days ago.
How long will you stay
here?
May be just for one week.

When will you leave for
Singapore?
I am scheduled to leave
tomorrow.
When will you get back?

I don't know yet.
May be I will go to Thai-
land from Singapore.

Then I will be back in
Malaysia.
Then you'll leave for
Japan?
I am not sure yet.
I have a lot of things to
do here.

JADUAL PERJALANAN

Bilakah anda tiba di
Kuala Lumpur?
Saya tiba 3 hari yang lalu.
Berapa lama anda akan
tinggal di sini?
Barangkali hanya untuk
1 minggu.
Bilakah anda akan ber-
angkat ke Singapura?
Menurut jadual, saya akan
berangkat besok.
Bilakah anda akan ber-
angkat balik?
Belum tahu lagi.
Barangkali saya akan terus
ke Thailand dari Singa-
pura.
Kemudian saya akan
kembali ke Malaysia.
Kemudian anda akan ber-
angkat ke Jepun?
Saya belum pasti lagi!
Banyak perkara yang
harus saya kerjakan di
sini.

If everything is okay, I'll go home.

You do seem to be awfully occupied.

Kalau semuanya selesai saya akan pulang.

Nampaknya anda sangat sibuk.

SIXTY-NINTH LESSON

FOOD IN THE RESTAURANT

Where shall we have lunch?

We shall have lunch at the Padang restaurant.

We shall have dinner just at home.

Let me see the menu.

You better order yourself.

What do you want to order?

I want to have fried rice.

With what?

Fried rice with omelette.

PELAJARAN KEENAM PULUH SEMBILAN

MAKANAN DI RESTORAN

Di mana kita akan makan tengahari?

Kita akan makan di restoran Padang.

Kita akan makan malam di rumah saja.

Mari saya lihat menu makanannya.

Lebih baik encik saja yang memesan.

Apa yang encik hendak pesan?

Saya ingin makan nasi goreng.

Nasi goreng dengan apa?

Nasi goreng dengan telur dadar.

After that I shall have fruits.	Selepas itu saya mahu makan buah-buahan.
I am starving (very hungry).	Saya sangat lapar.
I am very thirsty, too.	Saya juga sangat dahaga.
What do you want to drink?	Encik hendak minum apa?
I want to drink some coffee.	Saya hendak minum kopi.
As for me I want to drink some tea.	Saya pula ingin minum teh.

## SEVENTY-FIRST LESSON	## PELAJARAN KETUJUH PULUH SATU
### TRAVEL (I)	### MELANCONG (I)
Where do you stay in Kuala Lumpur?	Di Kuala Lumpur encik menginap di mana?
I usually stay at Hotel Merdeka.	Biasanya di Hotel Merdeka.
I prefer to stay at Merlin Hotel.	Saya lebih suka tinggal di Hotel Merlin.
There is also a zoo in Kuala Lumpur.	Di Kuala Lumpur juga ada zoo.
It is located at Ulu Kelang, Selangor.	Letaknya di Ulu Kelang, Selangor.
Have you visited the Lake Garden?	Sudahkah encik mengunjungi Taman Tasik?

Not yet. Let's go together.	Belum. Mari kita pergi bersama-sama.
I want to see Taman Bunga.	Saya ingin melihat Taman Bunga.
Well, the park has been restored.	Ya, sekarang taman itu telah dibaiki.
Tomorrow we shall go to Frasers Hill.	Besok kita akan pergi ke Bukit Fraser.
It is very cool over there.	Di sana hawanya sejuk sekali.
We can play golf there.	Kita boleh main golf di sana.
The next day we shall go to Penang.	Keesokan harinya baru kita ke Pulau Pinang.
Now the snake temple is being restored.	Kini tokong ular itu sedang dibaiki.
Don't forget to buy nutmeg in Penang.	Jangan lupa beli buah pala di Pulau Pinang.

SEVENTY-SECOND LESSON	PELAJARAN KETUJUH PULUH DUA
TRAVEL (II)	**MELANCONG (II)**
When are you going to Bali?	Bilakah encik akan ke Bali?
Maybe the day after tomorrow.	Mungkin lusa.

There, we can visit Putri Besakih.	Di sana kami akan mengunjungi Putri Besakih.
We can watch various dances.	Kami akan melihat berbagai-bagai tarian.
Kecak dance is quite popular.	Tarian kecak sangat popular.
Balinese girls are pretty.	Gadis Bali manis-manis.
We take a stroll on Sanur Beach.	Kami bersiar-siar di Pantai Sanur.
The girls are carrying offerings.	Gadis-gadis itu membawa sajian.
It is said to be for gods.	Dikatakan untuk dewa-dewa.
Where do you stay?	Di mana tuan menginap?
At Pertamina Cottage.	Di Pertamina Cottage.
Tomorrow we will go to Kintamani.	Besok kami akan ke Kintamani.
We will visit Tampak Siring Palace.	Kami akan mengunjungi istana Tampak Siring.
We can go by taxis or motorcycles.	Kita akan pergi dengan teksi atau motosikal.
We can rent motorcycles.	Kita boleh menyewa motosikal.

SEVENTY-THIRD LESSON

PLEASURE (I) – BALI

Have you ever seen cock-fighting?

There's cock-fighting in Bali.

It is a cruel act.

There's also cremation in Bali.

Only the corpses of the rich are burned.

It costs a lot of money, doesn't it?

The corpses of the poor are usually buried.

Quite a few of Balinese girls get married to foreigners.

We'll watch kecak dance in Bali.

Kecak dance is very interesting.

It seems to be of religious character.

As a matter of fact, most of Balinese dances are of religious character.

PELAJARAN KETUJUH PULUH TIGA

HIBURAN (I) – BALI

Pernahkah anda melihat laga ayam?

Di Bali ada laga ayam.

Itu perbuatan yang kejam.

Di situ juga ada pembakaran mayat.

Yang dibakar biasanya mayat orang-orang kaya.

Ia melibatkan perbelanjaan yang banyak bukan?

Mayat orang miskin biasanya dikuburkan saja.

Gadis-gadis Bali banyak yang berkahwin dengan orang asing.

Di Bali kita akan menonton tarian kecak.

Tarian kecak sangat menarik.

Ia merupakan upacara agama.

Sebenarnya, kebanyakan tarian Bali berkait rapat dengan agama.

Balinese culture is closely related to religion.	Kebudayaan Bali bertalian erat dengan agama.
Bali is also called demi-paradise.	Bali disebut juga sebagai separuh syurga.
It is a land of dreams for the tourists.	Ia merupakan impian pelancong-pelancong.

SEVENTY-FOURTH LESSON

PLEASURE (II) – BALI

Let's go to see sendratari.

What Sendratari?
Sendratari Ramayana.
Where is it?
At Prambanan Temple.
What time does the performance begin?
Performance usually begins at 9:30 p.m.
What time shall we start?

Right now.
Sendratari is a dramatic dance.

PELAJARAN KETUJUH PULUH EMPAT

HIBURAN (II) – BALI

Mari kita pergi menonton sendratari.

Sendratari apa?
Sendratari Ramayana.
Di mana tempatnya.
Di candi Prambanan.
Pukul berapa pementasan bermula?
Pementasan biasanya bermula pukul 9.30 malam.
Pukul berapa kita berangkat?

Sekarang juga.
Sendratari itu adalah seni drama dan tari.

Sendratari tells a story without using words.	Sendratari mengisahkan sebuah cerita tanpa menggunakan kata-kata.
A group of dancers stage Sendratari.	Sekumpulan penari mementaskan Sendratari.
They dance graciously.	Mereka menari dengan lemah gemalai.
They wear artistic dresses.	Pakaian mereka sangat artistik.
The spectators seems to be very happy.	Para penonton kelihatan sangat gembira.

SEVENTY-FIFTH LESSON

COMPARISON (I)

Mr. Smith speaks like a Malaysian.	Encik Smith bercakap seperti orang Malaysia.
Mr. Smith looks like an Arabian.	Rupa Encik Smith seperti orang Arab.
Mr. Smith's nose is pointed.	Hidung Encik Smith mancung.
That man is running like a horse.	Orang itu berlari seperti kuda.
He looks like an Arabian in that clothes.	Dia kelihatan seperti seorang Arab dalam pakaian itu.

PELAJARAN KETUJUH PULUH LIMA

PERBANDINGAN (I)

Money is running like water.	Wang mengalir seperti air.
He can speak foreign languages.	Dia boleh berbahasa asing.
Mr. Smith is as tall as Mr. Wong.	Encik Smith setinggi Encik Wong.
The girl is as beautiful as an angel.	Gadis itu secantik bidadari.
Her face is beautiful.	Mukanya cantik.
They look alike.	Rupa mereka serupa.
They are like brothers and sisters.	Mereka seperti adik dan kakak.
Tahu is as delicious as an egg.	Tahu itu seenak telur.
The orange is as sweet as sugar.	Limau itu manis seperti gula.
Tokyo is further than Manila.	Tokyo lebih jauh daripada Manila.
The Himalayas are higher than Alpines.	Banjaran Himalaya lebih tinggi daripada banjaran Alpine.
Kuala Lumpur is busier than Ipoh.	Kuala Lumpur lebih sibuk daripada Ipoh.

COMPARISON (II)

Tasik Titiwangsa is a quiet place.

He is wearing European clothes.

I eat a lot.

There are many books in my house.

He ate just a little, only a piece of bread.

I enjoy eating.

She has a melodious voice.

Liquor's very expensive.

Whiskey is stronger than wine and wine is stronger than beer.

His body is as cold as ice.

The soup is less warm.

Coffee is thick.

The house is very expensive.

Big towns have big population.

PERBANDINGAN (II)

Tasik Titiwangsa adalah tempat yang sunyi.

Dia berpakaian secara Eropah.

Saya makan banyak.

Di rumah saya ada banyak buku.

Dia makan sedikit, hanya sekeping roti.

Saya suka makan.

Suaranya merdu.

Minuman keras mahal sekali.

Wiski lebih keras daripada wain dan wain lebih keras daripada bir.

Badannya sesejuk ais.

Sup itu kurang panas.

Kopi itu sangat pekat.

Rumah itu sangat mahal.

Bandar besar banyak penduduknya.

The width of the street is the same.	Jalan itu sama lebarnya.
I am starving (very hungry).	Saya sangat lapar.
I want to eat first.	Saya mahu makan dulu.
I am thirsty, I want to drink ice water.	Saya haus, saya ingin minum ais.

<table>
<tr><td>SEVENTY-SEVENTH LESSON</td><td>PELAJARAN KETUJUH PULUH TUJUH</td></tr>
<tr><td>**LIVING**</td><td>**TEMPAT TINGGAL**</td></tr>
</table>

You used to live in Kuala Lumpur?	Encik pernah tinggal di Kuala Lumpur?.
Yes, I used to live there last year.	Ya, pernah setahun yang lalu.
Where do you live in Kuala Lumpur?	Di Kuala Lumpur encik tinggal di mana?
At Kampung Pandan.	Di Kampung Pandan.
Is Kuala Lumpur a big city?	Besarkah bandar Kuala Lumpur?
Yes, it is a big city. It has about 2 million inhabitants.	Ya, bandarnya besar, penduduknya kira-kira 2 juta orang.
Its airport is called Subang International Airport.	Lapangan terbangnya bernama Lapangan Terbang Subang.
Where's Hilton Hotel?	**Hotel Hilton di mana?**

At Jalan Tun Ismail.

Where's Globe Silks Store?

At Jalan Tuanku Abdul Rahman.

Where do you go shopping?

If you want to do shopping, please go to the Central Market, Jalan Chow Kit or Jalan Tuanku Abdul Rahman.

Is shopping at Central Market or Jalan Tuanku Abdul Rahman busy?

Di Jalan Tun Ismail.

Globe Silk Store di mana?

Di Jalan Tuanku Abdul Rahman.

Ke mana anda membeli-belah?

Kalau anda hendak mem-beli-belah pergilah ke Pasar Seni atau ke Jalan Chow Kit atau ke Jalan Tuanku Abdul Rahman.

Ramaikah orang di Pasar Seni atau Jalan Tuanku Abdul Rahman?

SEVENTY-EIGHTH LESSON

PELAJARAN KETUJUH PULUH LAPAN

PLACES OF INTEREST

TEMPAT-TEMPAT YANG MENARIK

What can you see at the museum?

We can see ancient articles there.

There's also a library at the museum.

Where's the aquarium?

Apakah yang dapat di-lihat di muzium?

Barang-barang lama.

Di muzium ada juga per-pustakaan.

Akuarium di mana?

At Pasar Ikan.

Di Pasar Ikan.

Where do you go for a movie?

Ke manakah anda pergi menonton?

At Cathay, at Jalan Bukit Bintang.

Di Cathay, di Jalan Bukit Bintang.

If you want to spend your weekend, where do you go?

Ke manakah anda pergi di hujung minggu?

You can go to Genting Highlands. It's cool there.

Tuan boleh pergi ke Genting Highlands. Udaranya sejuk.

Where can we stay at Genting Highlands?

Di mana kami boleh menginap di Genting Highlands?

You can stay at the hotel or rent a bungalow.

Encik boleh menginap di hotel atau menyewa bungalow.

Where else can you go for the weekend?

Ke mana lagi boleh kami pergi di hujung minggu?

To Fraser's Hill.

Ke Bukit Fraser.

At the Government Rest House.

Di Rumah Rehat Kerajaan.

Is it a good hotel? Yes, it is.

Baikkah hotel itu? Baik juga.

We usually go to Fraser's Hill by way of Kuala Lumpur.

Kami biasanya pergi ke Bukit Fraser melalui Kuala Lumpur.

VISITING (I)

Mr. Smith met Mr. Peterson in the sitting room.
They talked as follows:

"Good morning, Mr. Peterson."
"Good morning."
"Please sit down. Do you want to drink coffee?"
"There is coca-cola."
"Do you want fried rice or bread?"
"I usually have bread for breakfast."
"Where do you plan to go at the weekend?"

"I want to spend my weekend at Genting Highlands."
"Are you going alone?"

"No, not alone. I'll go with my friend."

MELAWAT (I)

Encik Smith berjumpa dengan Encik Peterson di bilik tamu.
Mereka berbual-bual seperti berikut:
"Selamat pagi Encik Peterson."
"Selamat pagi."
"Silakan duduk. Encik mahu minum kopi?"
Ada, coca-cola."
"Encik mahu nasi goreng atau roti?"
"Saya biasanya makan roti untuk sarapan."
"Akhir minggu ini encik merancang hendak ke mana?"
"Saya akan pergi ke Genting Highlands."

"Encik akan pergi sendirian?"
"Tidak, saya akan pergi dengan teman saya."

"Are you going there for your honeymoon?"
"No."
"With whom will you go?"

"Encik akan pergi ber-bulan madu?"
"Tidak."
"Dengan siapa?"

VISITING (II)

MELAWAT (II)

"How many nights will you spend there?"
"Just two nights. Sunday and Monday night."

"I will be back on Monday morning."
"It is nice, isn't it?"
"Will you go with me?"

"Thank you. Another time. I already have a previous appointment."
"Where are you going?"
"I am going to Bali, via Singapore."

"Berapa malam encik akan menginap di sana?"
"Dua malam saja. Malam Minggu dan malam Isnin."
"Hari Isnin pagi saya akan kembali."
"Elok juga, bukan?"
"Encik mahu ikut ber-sama-sama?"
"Terima kasih. Lain kali saja. Saya sudah ada rancangan lain."
"Encik mahu ke mana?"
"Saya akan ke Bali me-lalui Singapura."

"How are you going to Bali?"

"I am going by plane."

"Why are you going to Bali?"

"It is said that Bali is a beautiful island."

"Will you stop over at Singapore?"

"Yes, I will stop over at Singapore."

"Encik ke sana dengan apa?"

"Saya akan naik kapal terbang."

"Kenapa encik ke Bali."

"Orang mengatakan pulau Bali cantik sekali."

"Encik akan singgah di Singapura?"

"Ya, saya akan singgah di Singapura?"

THE EIGHTY-FIRST LESSON

TAXI (I)

Is this taxi occupied?

No, Sir.
Where are you going?
To the Railway Station.
I am leaving by the 5.30 train.
All right, Sir. Where is your baggage?
Over there, a suitcase and a bag.

PELAJARAN KELAPAN PULUH SATU

TEKSI (I)

Ada orangkah dalam teksi ini?

Tidak, encik.
Encik mahu ke mana?
Ke stesen keretapi.
Saya mahu naik keretapi jam 5:30.
Baik tuan. Mana barang-nya?
Di sana, sebuah beg dan beg bimbit.

Is there anybody seeing you off at the station?	Tidak adakah orang yang menghantarkan encik ke stesen?
No, there isn't.	Tidak ada.
This is the Railway Station.	Ini stesen keretapi, encik.
I'll use a porter.	
How much is the taxi fare?	Berapa tambang teksinya?
Three ringgit, Sir.	Tiga ringgit, encik.
This is a five dollar bill. Keep the change.	Ini wangnya lima ringgit. Tak payah pulangkan bakinya.
Thank you very much, Sir.	Terima kasih banyak-banyak, encik.

EIGHTY-SECOND LESSON	PELAJARAN KELAPAN PULUH DUA
TAXI (II)	**TEKSI (II)**
Take the suitcase!	Angkatlah beg itu.
Okay. Do you trust me?	Baiklah. Encik percaya pada saya?
Yes, I trust you.	Percaya.
Where is the train for Singapore?	Manakah keretapi ke Singapura?
There it is on the first track.	Itu encik, di platform satu.

How much is the ticket to Singapore?

Berapa harga tiket keretapi ke Singapura?

First class is $58.00, second class is $45.00 including a bed.

Kelas satu $58.00, kelas dua $45.00, termasuk tempat tidur.

One first class ticket, please!

Beri satu tiket kelas satu.

What time will we arrive in Singapore?

Jam berapa kami sampai di Singapura?

At 7 a.m.

Jam 7 pagi.

What is the distance between Singapore and Kuala Lumpur?

Berapa jaraknya antara Singapura dan Kuala Lumpur?

About 300 km.

Kira-kira 300 km.

Are there any vehicles waiting for you at the station?

Adakah kenderaan menunggu di stesen?

Yes, there are many vehicles, Sir.

Ada, banyak, encik.

THE EIGHTY-THIRD LESSON

PELAJARAN KELAPAN PULUH TIGA

SHOWS (I)

PERTUNJUKAN (I)

Sir, would you like to watch Dikir Barat?

Encik tidak ingin menonton Dikir Barat?

Oh, I watch quite often.

Oh, saya sudah sering menontonnya.

Call Mr. Hassan, he has never seen it.	Ajak Encik Hasan, dia belum pernah menontonnya.
Mr. Hassan would like to watch Dikir Barat?	Encik Hasan ingin pergi menonton Dikir Barat?
I would like too.	Ingin juga.
Come let's go together.	Mari kita pergi bersama-sama.
Where is it being held?	Di manakah ia diadakan?
At the Town Hall.	Di Dewan Orang Ramai.
Woh, that's good. Come. I will follow you.	Wah, itu bagus. Marilah saya temani encik.
What time shall we leave?	Pukul berapa kita berangkat?
At 8.30, after dinner.	Pukul 8:30, sesudah makan malam.
What time is the show?	Pukul berapa pertunjukan dimulai?
At 9.30 p.m.	Pukul 9:00 malam.
How are we going?	Kita naik apa?
We'll take a taxi.	Kita ambil teksi sahajalah.
Come let's go, it's time already.	Marilah kita berangkat, sekarang sudah waktunya.

SHOWS (II)

PERTUNJUKAN (II)

Have you booked a seat?	**Sudahkah anda menempah tempat duduk?**
Yes, I have booked a seat.	**Ya, saya sudah tempah tempat.**
May I come in?	**Boleh saya masuk?**
Yes, please sit down in row A.	**Boleh, sila duduk di baris A.**
May I smoke here?	**Bolehkah saya merokok di sini?**
Yes, certainly.	**Tentu boleh.**
May I take photographs?	**Bolehkah saya mengambil foto?**
It is allowed from here but not from there.	**Dari sini boleh, dari sana tidak boleh.**
We admire this show.	**Kami kagum dengan pertunjukan ini.**
Are you allowed to drink whiskey?	**Adakah anda dibenarkan minum wiski?**
I am not allowed to drink whiskey.	**Saya tidak dibenarkan minum wiski.**
I am afraid I might be drunk.	**Saya takut mabuk.**
Who prohibits you from whiskey?	**Siapa yang melarang?**
The doctor does.	**Doktor yang melarang.**

Why?...	Kenapa dilarang?
I used to suffer from serious illness.	Saya pernah sakit kuat.
May I come to your office tomorrow?	Boleh saya datang ke pejabat anda besok?
Do come, please.	Silakan datang!
What time will you be in your office?	Pukul berapa anda di pejabat?

EIGHTY-FIFTH LESSON	PELAJARAN KELAPAN PULUH LIMA
### TRIP	### PERJALANAN
I have to arrange my trip.	Saya harus aturkan perjalanan saya.
What time should you be at the airport?	Pukul berapa encik harus berada di lapangan terbang?
I must be at the airport at six.	Pukul 6 saya mesti berada di lapangan terbang.
Who will take you to the airport?	Siapakah yang menghantarkan encik ke lapangan terbang?
Nobody.	Tiada siapa.
What time will the plane take off?	Pukul berapa kapal terbang berangkat?
At seven, I must get up at five;	Pukul 7 pagi, saya harus bangun pukul 5 pagi.

You haven't paid the hotel bill yet?	Encik belum membayar sewa hotel?
Not yet, I will pay it.	Belum, saya akan membayarnya sekarang.
Until what date should I pay for the hotel?	Sampai tarikh bila saya harus membayar hotel?
Until the fifteenth of this month.	Hingga 15 haribulan ini.
How much must you pay?	Berapa encik harus membayar.
I must pay $200.00.	Saya harus membayar $200.00.

EIGHTY-SIXTH LESSON

ON THE PLANE

PELAJARAN KELAPAN PULUH ENAM

DALAM KAPALTERBANG

Should I report to the police?	Perlukah saya laporkan kepada polis?
No, you needn't.	Jangan, tidak perlu.
You have to show your passport to the immigration officials.	Encik harus menunjukkan pasport encik kepada pegawai imigresen.
Okay. What must I observe?	Baiklah, apa yang harus saya perhatikan?

During the take off you must fasten your seatbelt and don't smoke.

When the plane is already in the air, may I smoke?
Yes, of course.
(The stewardess smiles).
You must not smoke first.
No smoking.
After a little while you may smoke.
Why is it forbidden?
Because it is dangerous.
Can you speak Malay?

No, I can't.

Semasa hendak naik encik harus memakai tali pinggang dan jangan merokok.
Apabila berada di atas bolehkah saya merokok?
Tentu boleh. (Peramugari tersenyum).
Jangan merokok dulu.
Dilarang merokok.
Sebentar kemudian encik boleh merokok.
Kenapa dilarang?
Kerana merbahaya.
Encik boleh berbahasa Malaysia?
Tidak boleh.

EIGHTY-SEVENTH LESSON

PELAJARAN KELAPAN PULUH TUJUH

BEING ILL

SAKIT

I want to go to the doctor because I am sick.
Why didn't you come to the office yesterday?
I couldn't come to the office because I was sick.

Saya hendak pergi jumpa doktor kerana sakit.
Kenapa anda tidak datang ke pejabat semalam?
Saya tidak dapat datang ke pejabat kerana sakit.

Why did you fall ill? | Kenapa anda sakit?

I fell ill because I was very tired. | Saya sakit kerana terlalu penat.

Why did you become very tired? | Mengapa anda jadi terlalu penat?

Because I had to finish a hard job. | Kerana saya harus menyudahkan kerja yang berat itu.

So you have to take a rest now. | Oleh itu anda sekarang harus berehat.

All of them are sleeping, so don't talk loudly. | Mereka semua tidur, jangan bercakap kuat.

Why did they go to sleep so soon? | Apa sebabnya mereka lekas tidur?

Because they were very tired. | Kerana mereka terlalu letih.

Tomorrow is Sunday. So you can sleep till afternoon. | Besok hari Ahad, anda boleh tidur hingga tengahari.

I guess you can oversleep. | Saya percaya, anda biasa tidur lama.

EIGHTY-EIGHTH LESSON

PLAN

Please study carefully to pass the examination.

PELAJARAN LAPAN PULUH LAPAN

RANCANGAN

Rajin-rajinlah belajar, supaya lulus peperiksaan.

The youth must study.	Pemuda itu harus belajar.
If you want to go, please let me know.	Kalau anda hendak pergi beritahu saya.
If I pass the examination I will get a job.	Jika saya lulus saya akan dapat pekerjaan.
If it rains I will take an umbrella with me.	Jika hari hujan saya akan membawa payung.
I will not go because it is raining.	Saya tidak mahu pergi kerana hari hujan.
If you come here please bring my book with you.	Jika anda datang, tolong bawakan buku saya.
I will pick you up at the station when you arrive.	Saya akan menjemput anda di stesen setelah anda sampai.
I will have a party if I pass the test.	Saya akan adakan parti, jika saya lulus ujian.
He has been studying since morning.	Dia belajar semenjak pagi.
He will study until late at night.	Dia akan belajar sampai larut malam.
He reads the magazine before he goes to sleep.	Dia membaca majalah dulu sebelum tidur.
He brushes his teeth before going to sleep.	Dia gosok gigi sebelum tidur.
He washes his face after getting up.	Dia cuci muka sesudah bangun.

THE EIGHTY-NINTH LESSON

ALTHOUGH

He was successful because he worked hard.

Although he worked hard, he was not successful.

Having got a cold, I didn't take a bath.

I didn't buy the book because it was expensive.

I bought the book although it was expensive.

I will leave although he doesn't allow me.

He is very stingy, although he is rich.

Although he was late, he came.

Although it was Sunday, he went to the office.

Mr. and Mrs. Smith have arrived.

They are happy.

They attended the meeting.

PELAJARAN KELAPAN PULUH SEMBILAN

MESKIPUN

Kerana bekerja keras, dia telah berjaya.

Sungguhpun dia bekerja keras tetapi dia tidak berjaya.

Kerana selsema, saya tidak mandi.

Saya tidak beli buku itu kerana mahal.

Saya beli buku itu walaupun mahal.

Saya akan pergi walaupun dia melarang.

Sungguhpun dia kaya tetapi dia kedekut.

Walaupun dia terlambat, dia datang juga.

Walaupun hari Ahad, dia pergi ke pejabat.

Encik Smith serta isterinya sudah sampai.

Mereka gembira.

Mereka hadir di mesyuarat itu.

DISJUNCTIVE SENTENCES

The man is very rich, but he is still close fisted.

He is poor, yet, he is not stingy.

Mother's message is only this.

He has lived in the village since his childhood.

She is looking for her lost child.

The man is not only rich but also handsome.

The man is rich, but he is unhappy.

You may take coffee or tea or syrup.

You better come tomorrow to preside over the meeting.

You better take your jacket with you because it is cold.

You better wait patiently.

AYAT PERTENTANGAN

Orang itu sangat kaya, tetapi dia sangat kedekut.

Dia miskin, tetapi dia tidak kedekut.

Hanya inilah pesan ibu.

Semenjak kecil dia tinggal di desa.

Dia mencari anaknya yang hilang.

Orang itu bukan sahaja kaya, tetapi kacak.

Orang itu kaya, tetapi tidak bahagia.

Anda boleh minum kopi, teh atau sirap.

Lebih baik encik datang besok untuk mempengerusikan mesyuarat.

Lebih baik encik bawa jaket kerana hari dingin.

Lebih baik encik menunggu dengan sabar.

I prefer a late lunch.

Saya lebih suka makan lambat sedikit.

NINETY FIRST LESSON

PELAJARAN KESEMBILAN PULUH SATU

COURTESIES (I)

BERBUDI BAHASA (I)

Mr. Smith, have you had breakfast?

Encik Smith sudah sarapan pagikah?

Don't bother. Yes, I have had breakfast.

Jangan bimbang. Ya, saya sudah sarapan pagi.

What time did you get breakfast?

Pukul berapa encik bersarapan pagi?

At seven o'clock.

Pukul 7 pagi.

Have you had your lunch?

Sudahkah encik makan tengahari?

Not yet, I haven't had my lunch yet.

Belum, saya belum makan tengahari.

I will have lunch after a while.

Saya akan makan sebentar lagi.

There, Mr. Amin is eating.

Itu Encik Amin sedang makan.

Mr. Smith is eating too.

Encik Smith sedang makan juga.

Let's eat.

Mari kita makan.

Mr. Afandi, please eat!

Silakan makan, Encik Afandi.

Just a moment. Don't laugh while you eat!

I am still waiting for Mr. Hanafi.

I want to know the result of his talk.

I'll eat later on.

I'll eat now.

Please sit down!

Tunggu sebentar. Jangan tertawa ketika makan.

Saya masih menunggu Encik Hanafi.

Saya ingin tahu keputusan perbincangannya.

Saya akan makan kemudian.

Saya akan makan sekarang.

Silakan duduk.

NINETY-SECOND LESSON

COURTSIES (II)

I am still waiting for Mr. Hanafi.
Don't eat first!
Don't play with knife lest you get cut.
Wait for me a little while!
I'll get a lighter to smoke.

There is in the kitchen.
Let him eat first!

PELAJARAN KESEMBILAN PULUH DUA

BERBUDI BAHASA (II)

Saya masih menunggu Encik Hanafi.
Jangan makan dulu!
Jangan main pisau nanti luka.
Tunggu saya sebentar.
Saya akan ambil pemetik api untuk merokok.
Ada api menyala di dapur.
Biarlah dia makan dulu!

I got a letter from my elder brother.	Saya terima surat daripada abang saya.
Tell him to eat! Please eat!	Suruh dia makan. Sila makan!
He is eating while reading a newspaper.	Dia makan sambil membaca suratkhabar.
You better brush your teeth before going to sleep.	Sebaiknya anda menggosok gigi sebelum tidur.
Before I go to sleep, I brush my teeth.	Sebelum tidur, saya menggosok gigi.
Can you brush your teeth while whistling?	Bolehkah encik menggosok gigi sambil bersiul?
Yes, I can but to brush false teeth.	Boleh, jika menggosok gigi palsu.
When did you leave for Ipoh?	Pukul berapa encik berangkat ke Ipoh?
I left at 3 p.m.	Saya berangkat jam tiga petang.

NINETY-THIRD LESSON

PELAJARAN KESEMBILAN PULUH TIGA

FAVOURITES

KESUKAAN

During the rainy season, the road to Kg. Semarang is bad.

Semasa musim hujan, jalan ke Kg. Semarang menjadi becak.

Despite the dry season, the condition of the road has not improved.

There is summer, autumn, winter and spring in England.

Although the road is good, I prefer to go by train.

How may minutes will it take for you to walk from your house to the office?

It will take 25 minutes to walk.

How many minutes it will take you by bike?

About 10 minutes.

If you go by car?

Less than 5 minutes.

What will you do if you pass the examination?

I will work in my father's company.

Biarpun musim kemarau, keadaan jalan itu masih juga serupa.

Di Eropah ada musim panas, luruh, sejuk dan bunga.

Walaupun jalan baik, saya lebih suka naik keretapi.

Berapa minit encik ambil untuk berjalan dari rumah ke pejabat?

Kira-kira 25 minit.

Jika naik motosikal berapa minit?

Kira-kira 10 minit.

Jika naik kereta?

Tidak sampai lima minit.

Apa anda akan buat jika lulus peperiksaan itu?

Saya akan bekerja dalam perusahaan ayah saya.

NINETY-FOURTH LESSON

PASSIVE SENTENCES (I)

Who was the thief? I don't know.

Mr. Smith invited me to the party.

I was invited by Mr. Smith.

There is an invitation from Mr. Smith.

The servant swept the floor.

The floor was swept by the servant.

Please get a broom to sweep the floor.

The boy polished my shoes.

My shoes were polished by him.

I told the boy to polish my shoes.

Don't brush the shoes.

PELAJARAN KESEMBILAN PULUH EMPAT

AYAT PASIF (I)

Siapa pencuri itu? Saya tidak tahu.

Encik Smith mengundang saya ke majlis itu.

Saya diundang oleh Encik Smith.

Ada undangan dari Encik Smith.

Orang gaji itu menyapu lantai.

Lantai disapu oleh orang gaji itu.

Ambillah penyapu untuk menyapu lantai.

Budak itu menggilap kasut saya.

Kasut saya digilapnya.

Saya menyuruh budak itu menggilap kasut saya.

Jangan gosokkan berus itu kepada kasut.

Please get a piece of cloth to polish the shoes.	**Ambillah kain penggilap kasut.**
The servant washed Mr. Smith's clothes.	**Orang gaji itu mencuci pakaian Encik Smith.**
Mr. Smith's clothes were washed by the servant.	**Pakaian Encik Smith dicuci oleh orang gaji itu.**
Mr. Smith told the servant to wash his clothes.	**Encik Smith menyuruh orang gaji itu mencuci pakaiannya.**
He got his clothes washed.	**Dia minta supaya pakaiannya dicuci.**

NINETY-FIFTH LESSON

PELAJARAN KESEMBILAN PULUH LIMA

BORROWING MONEY

MEMINJAM WANG

Mr. Hanafi used to borrow money.	**Encik Hanafi pernah meminjam wang.**
He used to borrow money from the bank.	**Dia pernah meminjam wang daripada bank.**
Have you lent money?	**Pernahkah anda meminjamkan wang?**
Yes, I have.	**Pernah.**
To whom?	**Kepada siapa?**
To my friend.	**Kepada kawan.**
How much was the loan?	**Berapa banyakkah pinjaman itu?**

Just five hundred ringgit.	**Hanya lima ratus ringgit.**
How long was the loan?	**Wang itu dipinjamkan untuk berapa lama?**
Only for one month.	**Hanya untuk satu bulan.**
How much is the loan interest in the bank?	**Pinjaman di bank berapa bunganya?**
Six percent (6%) a month.	**Enam peratus (6%) sebulan.**
Who is the borrower?	**Siapa peminjamnya?**
Mr. Amin (is).	**Encik Amin.**
Lend me one hundred ringgit.	**Pinjamkan saya seratus ringgit.**
The boy climbed the coconut tree.	**Budak itu memanjat pokok kelapa**
Please climb the tree!	**Panjatlah pokok itu!**
Please climb.	**Silakan memanjat.**

NINETY-SIXTH LESSON	PELAJARAN KESEMBILAN PULUH ENAM

PASSIVE SENTENCES	AYAT PASIF (II)

Don't climb up and down lest you fall down.	**Jangan panjat-memanjat nanti jatuh.**
All my mangoes have been stolen by the boy.	**Habis buah manggaku dicuri oleh budak itu.**
The baboon can climb very well.	**Beruk itu boleh memanjat dengan baik sekali.**

The children climbed up and down.

Budak-budak itu bermain panjat-memanjat.

He is a coconut plucker.

Dia seorang pemanjat kelapa.

Tell him to climb the coconut tree.

Suruh budak itu memanjat pokok kelapa itu.

I wrote a letter to my parents.

Saya menulis surat kepada orang tua saya.

The letter was written in Bahasa Malaysia.

Surat itu ditulis dalam Bahasa Malaysia.

This paper is blank.

Kertas ini tidak bertulis.

My handwriting is not good.

Tulisan saya tidak cantik.

The writer has written many books.

Penulis itu banyak menulis buku.

I write with my pen.

Saya menulis dengan pen saya.

I am writing a letter to my father.

Saya menulis surat untuk ayah saya.

The book is in Arabic.

Buku itu ditulis dalam bahasa Arab.

107

USE OF PREPOSITIONS	PENGGUNAAN KATA DEPAN (I)
Mr. Yamada is sitting on a bench.	Encik Yamada duduk di atas bangku.
His dog is under the bench.	Anjingnya duduk di bawah bangku.
Behind the bench there is a flower.	Di belakang bangku ada bunga.
In front of the bench there is a stone.	Di depan bangku ada batu.
What is there between Mr. Yamada and Mr. Hanafi?	Apakah yang ada di antara Encik Yamada dan Encik Hanafi?
There is a chair between them.	Di antara mereka ada kerusi.
He is diving in the water.	Dia terjun ke dalam air.
Mr. Smith is still in his room.	Encik Smith masih di dalam bilik.
Mr. Johnson is waiting for him outside.	Encik Johnson menunggunya di luar bilik.
Among the pupils there is a teacher.	Di antara murid-murid itu ada seorang guru.
He is coming through the front gate.	Dia datang melalui pagar depan.

We had to be examined by the customs.	Kami terpaksa melalui pemeriksaan kastam.
He is leaning against the wall.	Dia bersandar pada dinding.
The swimmer has come out of the water.	Perenang itu keluar dari dalam air.
I have received a letter from my elder brother.	Saya terima surat dari abang saya.
I sent a letter to my younger sister.	Saya mengirim surat kepada adik saya.

NINETY-EIGHTH LESSON

PELAJARAN KESEMBILAN PULUH LAPAN

USE OF PREPOSITIONS

PENGGUNAAN KATA DEPAN (II)

The picture is hanging on the wall.	Gambar itu tergantung pada dinding.
He cut the meat with a knife.	Dia memotong daging itu dengan pisau.
We live in Kuala Lumpur.	Kami tinggal di Kuala Lumpur.
The ship sailed along the coast.	Kapal itu belayar menyusur pantai.
I have the letter with me.	Surat itu ada pada saya.
He is looking at me.	Dia melihat ke arah saya.

We can see the top of the mountain from our window.

Dari jendela, kami boleh lihat puncak gunung itu.

How late will he study?

Sampai pukul berapa dia belajar?

Since when has he been in Kuala Lumpur?

Semenjak bila dia pindah ke Kuala Lumpur?

He works in order to eat.

Dia bekerja untuk makan.

No admittance except for adults.

Dilarang masuk kecuali orang dewasa.

Malaysia has fertile soil.

Malaysia tanahnya subur.

In Malaysia there is plenty of uncultivated land.

Di Malaysia masih banyak tanah kosong.

Malaysia produces rice, coffee, tea, rubber, nutmeg, copra, tobacco, wood, oil and tin.

Malaysia menghasilkan padi, kopi, teh, getah, cengkeh, kelapa, tembakau, kayu, minyak dan timah.

NINETY-NINTH LESSON

PELAJARAN KESEMBILAN PULUH SEMBILAN

TIME

WAKTU

What time is it now?

Pukul berapa sekarang?

It is nine o'clock.

Pukul sembilan.

It is half past nine.

Pukul sembilan setengah.

It is a quarter to ten.

Suku pukul sepuluh.

It is ten o'clock sharp.	Pukul sepuluh tepat.
It is a quarter past ten.	Pukul sepuluh suku.
It is six a.m.	Pukul enam pagi.
It is five p.m.	Pukul lima petang.
It is two to two.	Kurang dua minit pukul dua.
It is one to one.	Kurang satu minit pukul satu.
According to my watch, it has just struck twelve.	Menurut jam saya, baru saja pukul dua belas.
I don't know what time it is.	Saya tidak tahu pukul berapa sekarang.
It must be five o'clock.	Mungkin pukul lima.
It may be four o'clock.	Barangkali pukul empat.

ONE HUNDRETH LESSON

PHRASES (I)

PELAJARAN KESERATUS

UNGKAPAN-UNGKAPAN (I)

Beside the hotel.	Di sebelah hotel itu.
Close to the hotel.	Dekat hotel itu.
It's a short-walk from the hotel.	Dekat dengan hotel itu.
It is a long way from here (far from here).	Jauh dari sini.
It is near.	Dekat dari sini.

It is not so far from here.	**Tidak berapa jauh dari sini.**
To the west of the building.	**Di sebelah barat bangunan itu.**
In the north.	**Di utara.**
To the east of my house.	**Di sebelah timur rumah saya.**
At the bookstore (book shop).	**Di kedai buku.**
At the hindu Temple.	**Di kuil Hindu**
On land.	**Di darat.**
On the sea.	**Di laut.**
In the air.	**Di udara.**
In the sky.	**Di langit.**

ONE HUNDRED AND FIRST LESSON

PELAJARAN KESERATUS SATU

PHRASES (II)

UNGKAPAN-UNGKAPAN (II)

Where?	**Di mana?**
Everywhere.	**Di mana-mana.**
Anywhere.	**Di mana saja.**
Not anywhere.	**Tidak di mana-mana.**
At home.	**Di rumah.**
At school.	**Di sekolah.**
At the hotel.	**Di hotel.**
At the office.	**Di pejabat.**

At the post office.	Di pejabat pos.
At the police station.	Di balai polis.
At the (railway) station.	Di stesen keretapi.
At the airport.	Di lapangan terbang.
At the bank.	Di bank.
At the restaurant.	Di restoran.
At the university.	Di universiti.

ONE HUNDRED AND SECOND LESSON

PHRASES (III)

PELAJARAN KESERATUS DUA

UNGKAPAN-UNGKAPAN (III)

On the table.	Di atas meja.
In the room.	Di dalam bilik.
Under the chair.	Di bawah kerusi.
On the floor.	Di lantai.
On the wall.	Di dinding.
On the ceiling.	Di siling.
In the car.	Di dalam kereta.
In the street.	Di jalan raya.
At the street corner.	Di sudut jalan.
Across the street.	Di seberang jalan.
At the back of the hotel. (behind the hotel).	Di belakang hotel.
At the swimming pool.	Di kolam renang.
At the lobby.	Di lobi.

At the counter.	Di kaunter.
At the next window.	Di tingkap sebelah.

COMPOUNDS (I)	KATA MAJMUK (I)
To and fro.	Pergi dan balik.
To fall in love.	Mencintai.
To love somebody/to be in love with.	Menaruh hati/dalam percintaan.
Traffic.	Lalulintas.
Hospital.	Rumah sakit/Hospital.
Asylum.	Rumah sakit otak.
Prison.	Penjara.
Drugstore.	Stor perubatan.
Very beautiful.	Sangat cantik.
Fair.	Pasaria.
Black market.	Pasar gelap.
Restaurant.	Restoran.
Credentials.	Surat kepercayaan.
Holiday, a day off.	Hari cuti.
To revenge.	Membalas dendam.

COMPOUNDS (II)	KATA MAJMUK (II)
Sweet and gentle.	Lemah-lembut.
Badly destroyed.	Hancur-lebur.
Extremely beautiful.	Terlalu cantik.
Light green.	Hijau muda.

Dark red.	Merah tua.
Light blue.	Biru muda.
Dark blue.	Biru tua.
Dark green.	Hijau tua.
Black and blue.	Biru lebam.
Stubborn, obstinate, pig-headed.	Keras kepala.
Emptyheaded.	Otak udang.
Two-faced.	Muka dua.
Light-fingered.	Panjang tangan.
Brokenhearted.	Patah hati.
In despair, be downcast, despondent.	Putus asa.

ADVERBS (I)

KATA KETERANGAN (I)

Always.	Selalu.
Not always.	Tidak selalu.
Ever.	Pernah.
Never.	Tidak pernah.
Often.	Sering.
Frequently.	Seringkali
Sometimes.	Kadang-kadang.
Occasionally.	Kadangkala.
Rarely, seldom.	Jarang-jarang.
Generally, in general.	Pada umumnya.
Particularly, in particular.	Pada khususnya.
At once, simultaneously.	Serentak.

Consequtively, at a stretch.	Berturut-turut.
Continuously, incessantly.	Terus-menerus.

ADVERBS (II) — KATA KETERANGAN (II)

Suddenly.	Tiba-tiba.
All of a sudden.	Sekonyong-konyong.
Right now.	Sekarang juga.
Just now.	Tadi/Sebentar tadi.
Already.	Sudah, telah.
Shortly.	Sebentar lagi.
Recently.	Baru-baru ini.
Lately/of late.	Kebelakangan ini.
Immediately/without delay.	Dengan segera/Serta-merta.
Spontaneously.	Secara spontan.
Quickly.	Dengan cepat.
Slowly.	Perlahan-lahan.
Gradually, step by step.	Beransur-ansur.

PASSIVE SENTENCES (I)

AYAT PASIF (I)

This form has been filled.

Borang ini sudah diisi.

This letter has not been signed yet.

Surat ini belum ditanda-tangani.

The telegram has been sent.

Telegram itu sudah di-kirim.

This room is to let.

Bilik ini untuk disewakan.

This car is for sale.

Kereta ini untuk dijual.

This shirt has been washed.

Kemeja ini sudah dicuci.

This skirt has not been ironed yet.

Skirt ini belum diseterika.

Dinner has been served.

Makan malam sudah di-hidangkan.

Dinner is ready.

Makan malam sudah sedia.

The driver has been paid.

Pemandu itu sudah di-bayar.

This room has been cleaned.

Bilik ini sudah dibersih-kan.

The room is available.

Bilik telah disediakan.

The manager has been told.

Pengurus sudah diberi-tahu.

My departure has been put off.

Pemergian saya ditunda.

My passport has been visaed.

Pasport saya telah diberi visa.

PASSIVE SENTENCES (II)

AYAT PASIF (II)

This baggage will be examined.	Beg ini akan diperiksa.
This passport should be renewed.	Pasport ini harus diperbaharui.
Doctor will be called in.	Doktor akan dipanggil.
This car is to let.	Kereta ini akan disewakan.
This medicine must be taken.	Ubat ini mesti diambil.
The meeting will be held.	Mesyuarat akan diadakan segera.
You will be told later on/ They will let you know later on.	Encik akan diberitahu kemudian.
This egg will be boiled.	Telur ini akan direbus.
This noodle will be fried.	Mi ini akan digoreng.
This bread will be baked.	Roti ini akan dibakar.
This illness will be diagnosed.	Penyakit ini akan didiagnosiskan.
This illness will be cured.	Penyakit ini akan diubati.
Your car must be thoroughly overhauled.	Kereta encik harus diperbaiki seluruhnya.
Your shoes will be polished.	Kasut encik akan digilapkan.
You will be invited to join the party.	Encik akan diundang menghadiri parti itu.

PASSIVE SENTENCES (III)

AYAT PASIF (III)

The firm will be established as soon as possible.	**Firma itu akan ditubuhkan secepat mungkin.**
The road has been repaired.	**Jalan itu sudah diperbaiki.**
I have been introduced to him.	**Saya sudah diperkenalkan kepadanya.**
I will be introduced to Mr. A.	**Saya akan diperkenalkan kepada Encik A.**
Your baggage will be transported to the Hotel.	**Beg tuan akan diangkut ke Hotel.**
Your child will be accompanied by Miss Emmy Salim to the amusement park.	**Anak tuan akan ditemani Puan Emmy Salim ke taman hiburan.**
You will be fetched at the airport.	**Tuan akan dijemput di lapangan terbang.**
This car can be used.	**Kereta ini boleh digunakan.**
The rotten tooth will be extracted.	**Gigi yang rosak itu akan dicabut.**
The porter has been called.	**Porter sudah dipanggil.**
I have been told to see ou.	**Saya disuruh menemui anda.**

GLOSSARY MALAY – ENGLISH

– A –

abang	— elder brother
acara	— program; agenda
ada	— to exist; there (be)
ada-tidaknya	— presence-or-absence (of X)
keadaan	— situation
mengadakan	— to conduct (research, hearing, etc.); hold (meetings, shows, ect.)
adalah	— to be
adat	— tradition
adik	— younger brother/sister
agak	— rather
agama	— religion
keagamaan	— religious (matters, problems etc.)
agung	— great
keagungan	— greatness
mengagungkan	— to glorify
pengagungan	— glorification
ahli	— expert
keahlian	— expertise
air	— water
aja	— informal form for saja
ajak	— something to do with asking someone
mengajak	— to ask one (to do something together with the speaker)
ajar	— something to do with teaching or learning
ajaran	— teaching (of Islam, Buddha, etc.)
belajar	— to study
mengajar	— to teach

mengajarkan	— to teach (followed by the subject matter taught)
mempelajari	— to make a study (of X)
pelajar	— student (in general)
pelajaran	— lesson
aju	— something to do with moving up or forward
mengajukan	— to put forward
akan	— will; would
akhir	— end (of stories, classes, etc.)
akhirnya	— finally
akibat	— consequence
mengakibatkan	— to bring about a consequence result in
aku	— I; me; my
mengakui	— to acknowledge
alam	— nature; something to do with experiencing
mengalami	— to experience; go through
pengalaman	— experience
alamat	— (an) address
alangkah	— Interjective marker meaning "how (wonderful, marvelous, etc.)"
alasan	— (a) reason; excuse
alat	— tool; device
aljibra	— algebra
aman	— peace (of place)
keamanan	— peacefully
mengamankan	— to render peace to
pengamanan	— act of rendering peace
ambil	— something to do with taking
mengambil	— to take (from there to here)
mengambilkan	— to take (from there to here for someone)

anak	— child
analisis	— analysis
menganalisis	— to analyse
ancam	— something to do with threatening
mengancam	— to threaten
anda	— you; your
anduk	— towel
aneh	— strange; unusual
anggap	— something to do with considering
menganggap	— to consider (X to be Y)
anggaran belanja	— budget (of Institutional or national mature)
anggota	— member
keanggotaan	— membership
nganggur	— to have nothing to do; have no job
penganggur	— unemployed person
angka	— grade; number; figure
angka kelahiran	— birth figure
angka kematian	— death figure
angkat	— something to do with leaving or lifting
berangkat	— to depart
mengangkat	— to lift
mengangkati	— to lift repeatedly
pengangkatan	— lifting; appointment (to a job)
angkut	— something to do with transporting
mengangkut	— to transport
mengangkuti	— to transport repeatedly
anjing	— dog
antara	— inter; something to do with accompanying or delivering
antara-kota	— inter-city
mengantar (kan)	— to accompany; to deliver

122

menghantar pulang	— to take (X) home
antre	— to stand in line. (a) line (for tickets, paying things, etc.)
anut	— something to do with adhering to or following.
menganut	— to follow; adhere to
penganut	— follower; adherent
apa	— question marker; what
apa khabar	— how are you
berapa	— how many; how much
kenapa	— why
mengapa	— why
siapa	— who; whom
arah	— direction
arca	— statue (made of stone)
asal	— origin
berasal	— to come from; originate
asalkan	— provided that
asin	— salty
asing	— foreign; strange
orang asing	— foreigner
asli	— genuine; original
asrama	— dormitory
atap	— roof
atom	— atom
atribut	— attribute
atur	— something to do with arranging or regulating
mengatur	— to arrange; handle, take care of
peraturan	— regulation
awas	— something to do with watching

mengawasi	— to keep an eye on; supervise
ayam	— chicken

— B —

baca	— something to do with reading
bacaan	— reading (materials, books, etc.)
membaca	— to read
membacakan	— to read (for someone)
pembacaan	— (a) reading
bahagi	— something to do with dividing
bahagian	— portion; part
membahagi	— to divide
membahagikan	— to distribute
pembahagian	— distribution; dividing
bagai	— something to do with a variety
berbagai-bagai	— various
sebagai	— as (a teacher, artist, etc.)
bagaimana	— how
bagus	— good
bahan	— materials
bahan makanan	— foodstuff
bahan pokok	— basic needs/commodity
bahas	— something to do with analysing.
membahas	— to discuss in some detail
pembahas	— discussant
bahasa	— language
bahaya	— danger
berbahaya	— dangerous
bahawa	— that (as a conjunction)
baik	— good

baik-baik saja	— just fine
baiklah	— all right
baik-baiklah	— be good
memperbaiki	— to improve (X)
perbaiki	— improvement
bakar	— something to do with burning
membakar	— to burn (X)
membakari	— to burn (X) repeatedly
kebakaran	— to be caught on fire; fire
bakat	— talent
banding	— something to do with comparing
membandingkan	— to compare
bank	— bank
bangku	— bench, desk
bangsa	— nationality
bangun	— to wake up; something to do with building.
kebangunan	— awakening
membangun	— to build
membangunkan	— to wake up (X)
pembangunan	— development; building (of X)
banjir	— flood
kebanjiran	— to be flooded
membanjiri	— tò flood
bantah	— something to do with arguing
membantah	— to argue (against); deny
bantu	— something to do with helping
bantuan	— aid; help
membantu	— to help; assist; aid
pembantu	— helper; assistant
banyak	— many, much
kebanyakan	— majority (of)

bapa	— father;
barang	— thing
barangkali	— perhaps, maybe
barat	— west
baris	— line (of a page)
baru	— new; just (came, left, etc.).
batas	— border; limit
berbatas	— bordered
membatasi	— to limit
pembatasan	— limitation
perbatasan	— border
batin	— something to do with mental matters
kebatinan	— mysticism
batu	— stone
bawa	— something to do with bringing
membawa	— to bring (from here to there)
membawakan	— to bring (from here to there for someone)
bayang	— something to do with imagining
bayangan	— shadow
membayangkan	— to imagine
bayar	— something to do with paying
membayar	— to pay
bayi	— baby
bebas	— free
kebebasan	— freedom
membebaskan	— to free; set (X) free
pembebasan	— freeing
beberapa	— several
beca	— a three wheel public vehicle
beza	— something to do with differing
berbeza	— to be different

membezakan	— to differentiate
pembezaan	— differentiating; differentiation
perbezaan	— difference
begitulah	— like that
begitulah	— so so; not bad
bekas	— former (president, husband, etc.)
beku	— frozen
kebekuan	— state of being frozen
membeku	— to become frozen
membekukan	— to freeze (X)
pembekuan	— freezing of (X)
bela	— something to do with defending
membela	— to defend
pembela	— defender
belakang	— behind; rear
belanja	— something to do with shopping
berbelanja	— to do/go shopping
belas	— unit between ten and twenty
sebelas	— eleven
beli	— something to do with buying
membeli	— to buy
membelikan	— to buy (for someone)
beliau	— he/she; his/her; him/her (honorific)
belok	— to turn (left or right)
belum	— not yet
benar	— true; correct
membenarkan	— to allow
sebenarnya	— actually; in fact
benci	— hate
kebencian	— hatred
membenci	— to hate
bendahari	— treasurer

127

bentuk	— form shape; something to do with form-ing
berbentuk	— to have the form/shape
membentuk	— to form
berani	— brave; courageous
keberanian	— bravery; courage
beras	— uncooked rice
berat	— heavy
keberatan	— to object; mind
beres	— settled; taken care of
beri	— something to do with giving
memberi	— to give
memberikan	— to give (followed by the object given)
memberitahu	— to inform; let (X) know
pemberi	— provider; giver
berontak	— something to do with rebelling
memberontak	— to rebel
pemberontakan	— rebellion
bersih	— clean
kebersihan	— cleanliness
membersihkan	— to clean
pembersihan	— cleaning
besar	— big; large
membesar	— to become big
membesarkan	— to enlarge (X)
besok	— tomorrow
betapa	— Interjective marker meaning "how (beautiful, reat, etc.)"
betul	— correct; true
kebetulan	— by chance
membetulkan	— to correct; fix
sebetulnya	— actually. in fact

biar	— let (him go, eat, etc.)
membiarkan	— to let; tolerate
biasa	— usual; common
biasanya	— usually
luar biasa	— extraordinary
bicara	— something to do with talking
berbicara	— to talk
membicarakan	— to talk about; discuss
pembicaraan	— discussion
bidan	— midwife
bidang	— field (of study)
bijaksana	— wise
kebijaksanaan	— wisdom, policy
bimbang	— doubtful
kebimbangan	— doubt
bintang	— star
bintang filem	— movie star
Biro	— bureau
biru	— blue
bas	— bus
blok	— block
bocor	— to leak (in X leaks)
bodoh	— stupid
boleh	— may; be allowed to
botol	— bottle
buah	— a classifier for indefinite object
sebuah	— a (book; gift, etc.)
buang	— something to do with throwing away
membuang	— to throw away
buat	— something to do with making or behaving
berbuat	— to do
buatan	— product (of) (Japan, England, etc.)

membuat	— to make
membuatkan	— to make (for someone)
pembuatan	— making
perbuatan	— behaviour; deed
budaya	— something to do with culture
kebudayaan	— culture
buka	— something to do with opening
membuka	— to open (X)
pembuka	— opener
bukan	— not (followed by a noun)
bukannya	— not that (I dislike him, etc.)
bukan main	— Interjective marker meanings "how (wonderful, stupid, etc.)
buku	— book
buku tulis	— writing book
bukti	— proof; evidence
membuktikan	— to prove
bulan	— month; moon
bulu	— feather
bunga	— flower; interest form a bank)
bungkus	— something to do with wrapping
membungkus	— to wrap
membungkus	— to wrap (several things individually).
bunuh	— something to do with killing
terbunuh	— to get killed
buru	— something to do with hunting
berburu	— to do/go hunting
burung	— bird

– C –

cakap	— something to do with conversing
percakapan	— conversation
calon	— candidate; future (husband, wife, etc.)
kuil	— temple
cantik	— beautiful
capai	— something to do with reaching
mencapai	— to reach (a destination or level)
cara	— way; means; method
cari	— something to do with looking for
mencari	— to look for
catatan	— (a) note
cek	— cheque
celaka	— unlucky; unfortunate; darn it
kecelakaan	— accident; mishap
cemburu	— to be jealous
mencemburui	— to be jealous of
cengkam	— something to do with gripping
mencengkam	— to grip
cepat	— fast; quick
cerai	— something to do with divorcing
bercerai	— to be divorced
perceraian	— (a) divorce
cerdas	— intelligent
cerita	— story
bercerita	— to tell a story
jalan cerita	— (a) plot
menceritakan	— to narrate; tell
tema cerita	— theme
cetak	— something to do with printing
mencetak	— to print

131

cinta	— something to do with loving
mencintai	— to love
pencinta	— lover
cipta	— something to do with creating
ciptaan	— creation (of)
menciptakan	— to create
pencipta	— creator
cium	— something to do with kissing
mencium	— to kiss
menciumi	— to kiss repeatedly
cocok	— suitable; fit
colok	— something to do with poking or striking
menyolok	— to be striking; to poke
coret	— something to do with crossing out
mencoret	— to cross out (the wrong words)
mencoreti	— to cross out or scratch repeatedly
cuba	— something to do with triying
mencuba	— to try
percubaan	— experiment; trial
cuci	— something to do with washing
mencuci	— to wash
mencucikan	— to wash (for someone)
cukup	— enough; sufficient
culik	— something to do with kidnapping or abducting
menculik	
menculik	— to kidnap or abduct
curi	— something to do with stealing
kecurian	— to be stolen
mencuri	— to steal
curiga	— to be suspicious
mencurigai	— to be suspicious of; suspect

– D –

daerah	— area; region
daftar	— (a) list
mendaftarkan	— to list; register
pendaftaran	— registration
dagang	— something to do with commerce or business
berdagang	— to do private business (such as buying and selling things)
pedagang	— merchant
perdagangan	— commerce; trade
dakwa	— something to do with accusing
dakwaan	— accusation
mendakwa	— to accuse
dalam	— deep; profound; in
memperdalam	— to deepen
dalang	— puppeteer in wayang shows; mastermind
damai	— peaceful
berdamai	— to make peace
mendamaikan	— to bring peace; pacify
pendamai	— peace
dan	— and
dapat	— can; be able to; something to do with thinking or obtaining
berpendapat	— to be of opinion; think
mendapat	— to get; obtain
pendapat	— opinion
pendapatan	— income; result
pendapatan bersih	— net income
pendapatan kasar	— gross income

pendapatan per kapita	— per capita income
terdapat	— to be found
dapur	— kitchen
darat	— land (oppiste of se)
daratan	— (main) land
mendarat	— to land
mendaratkan	— to land (X)
pendaratan	— landing
dari	— from; of
dasar	— base; foundation
berdasarkan	— to be based on
data	— data
datang	— to come
kedatangan	— to be visited (by); arrival
mendatangi	— to come to (a place or person); approach
mendatangkan	— to bring in; summon; import
dekan	— dean
dekat	— near
mendekat	— to come near; draw near
mendekati	— to come near to; approach
mendekatkan	— to bring (X) closer
demokrasi	— democracy
demokrasi terpimpin	— guided democracy
demonstrasi	— demonstration
berdemonstrasi	— to demonstrate
dengan	— with; by
dengar	— something to do with hearing or listening
mendengar	— to hear
mendengarkan	— to listen to
depan	— front; next (week, month, etc.)

134

departmen	— department; ministry
derita	— something to do with suffering
menderita	— to suffer
penderitaan	— suffering
desa	— village
dewan	— council
di	— in; on; at
dia atau ia	— he/she; his/her; him/her
diam	— to be quiet; to dwell
kediaman	— residence
didik	— something to do with educating
mendidik	— to educate
pendidikan	— education
dingin	— cold
kedinginan	— to be chilled
diri	— something to do with standing or self
berdiri	— to stand
mendirikan	— to establish; erect; found
pendiri	— founder
doktor	— medical doctor
doktor falsafah	— Doctor of Philosophy
doktoranda (Dra.)	— similar to a master's degree (female)
doktorandus (Drs.)	— similar to a master's degree (male)
dokumen	— document
drama	— drama; play
dua	— two
duduk	— to sit; something to do with sitting
duduk-duduk	— to sit around
kedudukan	— position; situation
menduduki	— to sit on (X); occupy
mendudukkan	— to make (X) sit; place; put
penduduk	— inhabitant; population

pendudukan	— act of making (X) sit; placing; putting; occupation
dukun	— shaman; one wo does things super-taburally
dukun bayi	— traditional midwife
dukung	— something to do with supporting
mendukung	— to support (idea, proposal, etc.)
pendukung	— supporter
dunia	— world
dunia ramai	— real world
duta	— envoy
duta besar	— ambassador
kedutaan	— embassy

— E —

ekor	— tail
seekor	— classifier for animals
eksport	— export
mengeksport	— to export
ekstra	— extra
empat	— four
perempatan	— four way intersection
seperempat	— one fourth
enak	— delicious; pleasant; good
enam	— six
engkau	— you; your (not quite respectiful)

— F —

fakulti	— faculty; college (of education; engineering, etc.)
film	— film
falsafah	— philosophy

— G —

gadis	— (adult) girl; unmarried woman
gagah	— strong, full of strength.
gagal	— to fail; be unsuccessful
gajah	— elephant
gaji	— wage; salary
gali	— something to do with digging
menggali	— to dig; excavate
gambar	— (a) picture; drawing
gambaran	— illustration
menggambarkan	— to illustrate; describe
ganggu	— something to do with bothering
mengganggu	— to bother; disturb; tease
ganti	— something to do with replacing
menggantikan	— to replace
garaj	— garage
garpu	— fork
garuda	— eagle
gaul	— something to do with associating
bergaul	— to associate
gelas	— glass (for drinking)
gemar	— something to do with liking; be fond of
menggemari	— to be fond of; like very much

137

gembira	— to be glad; cheerful; happy
gemilang	— wonderful; brilliant
gereja	— church
gerak	— something to do with moving
gerakan	— movement (literal or figurative)
bergerak	— to move
pergerakan	— movement (figurative)
giat	— energetic; active
kegiatan	— activity
mempergiat	— to intensify; encourage
gigit	— something to do with biting
menggigit	— to bite
menggigiti	— to bite repeatedly
gila	— to be insance; crazy; crazy about
golong	— something to do with grouping
golongan	— group; class
golongan karya	— technocrat group
penggolongan	— grouping; classification
gong	— gong
goreng	— something to do with frying; fried
gotong royong	— concept of mutual help
gratis	— gratis
gudang	— storehouse
gula	— sugar
guna	— something to do with using
berguna	— to be useful
menggunakan	— to use; make use of
guru	— teacher

– H –

habis	— finished; all gone
kehabisan	— to run out of
penghabisan	— last; end
hadir	— something to do with being present
menghadiri	— to attend (not school)
hafal	— something to do with knowing by heart
menghafalkan	— to learn by heart; memorize
haji	— one who has made the pilgrimage to Mecca
hak	— (a) right
hal	— matter; case; thing (nonphysical)
halaman	— page; yard
halus	— refined; soft; gentle
hampir	— almost
hancur	— collapsed; shattered; destroyed
hanya	— only
harap	— something to do with hopping or expecting
mengharap(kan)	— to hope or expect
harga	— price
menghargai	— to appreciate; respect; price
penghargaan	— appreciation; respect
hari	— day
sehari-hari	— daily; every day
harus	— must; have to
hasil	— to produce
hasut	— something to do with agitating
menghasut	— to agitate
menghasuti	— to agitate repeatedly
hati	— heart

haus	— to be thirsty
kehausan	— to suffer from thirst
henti	— something to do with stopping
berhenti	— to stop
menghentikan	— to stop (X)
hias	— something to do with decorating
berhias	— to dress up; make up
menghias(i)	— to decorate
hidung	— nose
hidup	— to live; be alive
kehidupan	— life; livelihood
hijau	— green
hilang	— lost; missing
kehilangan	— to lose (X)
menghilang	— to disappear
menghilangkan	— to lose (X)
hormat	— respect; something to do with respecting
menghormati	— to respect
hotel	— hotel
hubung	— something to do with contacting
hubungan	— relationship; contact; communication
berhubungan	— connected
menghubungi	— to contact
hujan	— rain; to rain
hukum	— law
hukuman	— sentence; punishment
menghukum	— to punish; sentence
hutang	— debt

— I —

ia atau dia	— he/she; his/her; him/her
ibu	— mother
ibukota	— capital; city
ikan	— fish
perikanan	— fishery
ikut	— something to do with following
mengikuti	— to follow
ilmu	— knowledge; science
imigrasi	— immigration
import	— import
mengimport	— to import
inap	— something to do with sleeping
menginap	— to spend the night; stay over
indah	— beautiful (of panorama)
industri	— industry
perindustrian	— industry; industrial (affairs); industralization
infiltrasi	— infiltration
kadar inflasi	— inflation rate
Inggeris	— English; British
ingin	— to desire; would like to
keinginan	— (a) desire
menginginkan	— to disire; wish
ini	— this
instansi	— agency; organ
antarabangsa/	— international
irama	— rhythm
isi	— contents
berisi	— to contain

mengisi	— to fill (up/in)
mengisikan	— to fill (for someone)
istana	— palace
istirehat	— (a) rest; to rest
isteri	— wife
itu	— that; the

— J —

jadi	— so; therefore
menjadi	— to become
menjadikan	— to make (X) become
tidak jadi apa	— it does not matter
tidak jadi	— cannot make (the movie, meeting, etc.)
jaga	— something to do with guarding
menjaga	— to guard; keep watch
penjaga	— guard
penjaga pintu	— doorman
jahat	— wicked; evil
kejahatan	— crime
jahit	— something to do with sewing
menjahit	— to sew
menjahitkan	— to sew (for someone)
jajah	— something to do with occupying
jajahan	— colony
menjajah	— to colonialize
penjajahan	— occupation; colonialization
jalan	— street; something to do with walking
berjalan	— to walk
berjalan-jalan	— to take a walk
jalan cerita	— (a) plot

menjalankan	— to operate; carry out
perjalanan	— journey; trip
jam	— o'clock; hour
jamin	— something to do with guaranteeing
terjamin	— guaranteed
janji	— (a) promise
berjanji	— to promise
perjanjian	— agreement
jangan	— don't
jarang	— seldom
jatuh	— to fall, fail (in exam)
kejatuhan	— (the) fall; struck by a falling (X)
menjatuhi	— to fall on (X)
menjatuhkan	— to let fall; make (X) fall; topple
jauh	— far
menjauh	— to go farther away
menjauhi	— to stay away from; avoid
menjauhkan	— to keep (X) away from (Y)
jawab	— something to do with responding
jawaban	— response; answer
menjawab	— to respond; answer
jelas	— clear; obvious
jelik	— bad; ugly
jemput	— something to do with picking up
menjemput	— to pick up
menjemputi	— pick up (more than once)
penjemputan	— (the) pick up
jendela	— window
jual	— something to do with selling
menjual	— to sell
menjual	— to sell (things more than once)
menjualkan	— to sell (for someone)

juang	— something to do with struggling
berjuang	— to struggle (for national cause)
perjuangan	— struggle (for independence , life, etc.)
juga	— also
Julai	— July
Jumaat	— Friday
jumlah	— total
berjumlah	— to have the total of
menjumlahkan	— to total (X)
Jun	— June
juru	— something to do with vocational abilities
sekolah vokesyenal	— vocational school
jurusan	direction; field of study
juta	— million

— K —

khabar	— news
apa khabar?	— how are you?
kabinet	— cabinet (of ministers)
kabur	— vague; gone
kaca	— glass; mirror
kacau	— messy; confused; in disorder
kekacauan	— (a) mess; confusion; disorder
mengacau	— to stir up (X); to confuse; cause disorder
pengacau	— trouble maker
pengacauan	— riot; disturbance; rebellion of a less serious nature
kadangkala	
kadang-kadang	— sometimes
kagum	— to be amazed; impressed
mengkagumi	— to admire

mengkagumkan	— to amaze; be amazing
kan	— question particle
kain	— fabrics; cloth
kakak	— elder sister
kaki	— leg; foot (also for measurement)
kalah	— defeated; lost
mengalahkan	— to defeat; beat
kali	— times (in multiplication)
kalau	— if, when
kami	— we; us; our (exclusive)
Khamis	— Thursday
kamu	— you (not quite respectful)
kanan	— right (opposite of left)
kapal	— ship
kapal terbang	— aeroplane
perkapalan	— shipping
kapur	— chalk
karang	— something to do with composing or writing
karangan	— composition; article; writing
mengarang	— to compose; write
pengarang	— writer; author
kerana	— because
kad	— card
karya	— work (usually of art)
kasihan	— it's pity; too bad
kata	— word; something to do with saying
berkata	— to say; talk
katanya	— they say
mengatakan	— to say (X)
perkataan	— word

kaum	— plural form used before a group of people
kawal	— something to do with escorting
mengawal	— to escort
kahwin	— to be married; something to do with marrying
mengahwini	— to marry (X)
mengahwinkan	— to marry off
perkahwinan	— marriage, wedding
kaya	— rich
kekayaan	— wealth
ke	— to; toward; particle for ordinal numbers
kebaya	— Javanese blouse
kebun	— garden
perkebunan	— plantation
kecil	— small; little
mengecil	— to become small/little
mengecilkan	— to make (X) small/little
memperkecil	— to make (X) smaller
kehendak	— desire; wish
kekasih	— sweetheart; beloved
kelas	— class
keliling	— something to do with going around
mengelilingi	— to go around (X)
mengelilingkan	— to make take (X) go around
keluarga	— family
kemari	— (to) here
kelmarin	— yesterday
kembali	— you're welcome (after thank you); something to do with returning; to come back
mengembalikan	— to return (X)

kembang	— something to do with blooming or developing
berkembang	— to bloom; develop
mengembangkan	— to develop (X)
pengembangan	— (the) developing of (X)
perkembangan	— development
kemudi	— steering wheel
mengemudikan	— to steer drive; lead
kemudian	— then; afterward
kenal	— to be acquainted; something to do with knowing
mengenalkan	— to introduce; let (X) known
perkenalan	— introduction
kenderaan	— transport
kenyang	— to be full (of food)
kepada	— to (a person)
kepala	— head (literal and figurative)
mengepalai	— to head
kera	— monkey
keras	— hard (of physical things); alcoholic (drink etc.); serious
kereta	— carriage
keretapi	— (a) train
keretapi barang	— cargo car/train
keretapi penumpang	— passanger train
kering	— dry
mengering	— to become dry
mengeringkan	— to dry (X)
kerja	— something to do with working
bekerja	— to work
bekerjasama	— to work together; cooperate

mengerjakan	— to do (X)
pekerjaan	— job; work
kertas	— paper
kertas tulis	— writing paper
keruh	— muddy; turbid
mengeruh	— to become muddy/turbid
mengeruhkan	— to make (X) muddy/turbid
kesan	— impression
mengesan	— to be impressive
ketika	— when (of past action)
khusus	— special; especially
kilo	— kilogram; kilometre
kira	— something to do with guessing; thought (he was coming, etc.)
kira-kira	— approximately
mengira	— to guess; suspect; think; thought
kiri	— left (opposite of right)
kirim	— something to do with sending
kiriman	— whatever one sends (package, letter, etc.)
mengirim	— to send
mengirimi	— to send (followed by a person)
mengirimkan	— to send (followed by a thing)
pengiriman	— (the) sending
kita	— we; us; our (inclusive)
klinik	— clinic
kolam renang	— swimming pool
kolot	— orthodox; conservative
komunis	— communist
konsep	— concept
kontrol	— something to do with controlling
koordinasi	— coordination
mengkoordinasikan	— to coordinate

148

kopi	— coffee
korban	— victim
kosong	— empty
kekosongan	— emptiness
mengosongkan	— to empty (X)
pengosongan	— (the) emptying
kota	— city; town
kotor	— dirty
kritik	— something to do with civing; civiticism
kuasa	authority; power
berkuasa	— to be in power; rule
kekuasaan	— authority; power
menguasai	— to control; dominate
kuat	— strong
kucing	— cat
kuda	— horse
kuli	— labourer
kuliah	— to attend a university; university course
kulit	— leather
wayang kulit	— Javanese shadow show; Javanese puppet
kumpul	— something to do with gathering
berkumpul	— to gather
kumpulan	— collection; association; gathering
mengumpulkan	— to gather (X). collect
pengumpulan	— (the) collecting
perkumpulan	— association
kunci	— key (literal and figurative)
kuning	— yellow
kunjung	— something to do with visiting
mengunjungi	— to visit
pengunjung	— visitor

kuno	— ancient
kurang	— less; not enough
kekurangan	— to run out of
mengurangi	— to reduce
kerusi	— chair
khuatir	— to be worried
kiyai	— a man knowledgeable in Islamic matters

– L –

lagi	— again; more
lagu	— song
lagu kebangsaan	— national anthem
lahir	— to be born
melahirkan	— to give birth to
dilahirkan	— to be born
lain	— other; different
lain kali	— some other time
laksana	— as; something to do with carrying out
melaksanakan	— to carry out; implement
pelaksanaan	— implementation
laku	— something to do with doing
berlaku	— to be valid; in force
melakukan	— to do (X)
lalu	— afterwards; past/last (week, month, etc.)
lalu-lintas	— traffic
lama	— old (of time); long (of time)
lambang/simbol	— symbol
lambat	— slow
terlambat	— late

langsung	— straight; direct; something to do with taking place
berlangsung	— to take place
lantik	— something to do with inaugurating
melantik	— to inaugurate
perlantikan	— inauguration
lapangan/bidang	— field (also of study)
lapangan terbang	— airport
lapar	— to be hungry
kelaparan	— to starve
lapor	— something to do with reporting
laporan	— (a) report
melaporkan	— to report
larang	— something to do with forbidding
melarang	— to forbid
terlarang	— forbidden
latih	— something to do with practicing
berlatih	— to practice
latihan	— (a) practice
lawan	— something to do with apposing
melawan	— to oppose
perlawanan	— opposition
layar	— sail
layan	— something to do with serving
melayani	— to serve; entertain (guests, etc.); walt on
pelayan	— servant; waiter/waitress
pelayanan	— service
layar	— screen; curtain; sail
lebih	— more
lebih dari (pada)	— more than
leher	— neck
lempar	— something to do with throwing

151

melempar	— to throw
melempari	— to throw (at)
melemparkan	— to throw (with)
lengkap	— complete
melengkapi	— to equip; furnish
lenyap	— vanished
lepas	— something to do with releasing
melepaskan	— to let go; release
letak	— something to do with locating or placing
terletak	— to be located
letus	— something to do with erupting
meletus	— to erupt; explode; break out
lewat	— via; by way of
libur	— something to do with vacationing
liburan	— vacation; holiday
lihat	— something to do with seeing or showing
kelihatannya	— it looks; it seems
melihat	— to see
melihat-lihat	— to look around
penglihatan	— sight
lima	— five
lincah	— energetic lively; active (usually of little children)
lindung	— something to do with protecting
melindungi	— to protect
loket	— ticket window; counter
lompat	— something to do with jumping
melompat	— to jump
melompati	— to jump (over X)
melompatkan	— to let jump; make (X) jump
luar	— out; outside
luar biasa	— extraordinary

luar negeri	— foreign country; abroad
mengeluarkan	— to issue; expell
pengeluaran	— expenditure; issuance
luas	— wide; extensive; broad
meluas	— to become wide/extensive/broad
meluaskan	— to widen (X)
memperluas	— to further widen (X)
lucu	— humorous; funny
lukis	— something to do with (art) painting
lukisan	— (art) painting
melukis	— to paint
lulus	— to pass (of exams)
lumayan	— moderate; not too much but not too little either
lupa	— to forget
lusa	— day after tomorrow

– M –

maaf	— to be sorry; (a) pardon; excuse (me, I have to go.... etc.)
macam	— kind; type
mahal	— expensive
mahasiswa	— university student
main	— something to do with playing
main ke rumah	— to come and see (us, etc.)
memainkan	— to play (X)
pemain	— player
permainan	— game
majalah	— journal; magazine
maju	— developed; to progress

kemajuan	— (a) progress
memajukan	— to advance (X); put forward
makan	— to eat
bilik makan	— dining room
makanan	— food
makan malam	— to have dinner; dinner
makan pagi	— to have breakfast; breakfast
makan tengahari	— to have lunch; lunch
memakan waktu	— to consume time; take time
makin	— increasingly; the more
makmur	— prosperous
kemakmuran	— prosperity
malah	— on the contrary
malam	— evening; night
malas	— lazy
malu	— to be embarrassed; shy
memalukan	— to embarras (X); be embarrassing
mana?	— where?
bagaimana?	— how?
bilamana?	— when (of time)?
dari mana?	— (from) where?
di mana?	— (at) where?
di mana-mana?	— (at) anywhere?
ke mana?	— (to) where?
mandi	— to take a bath/shower
memandikan	— to bathe (X)
manis	— sweet (literal and figurative)
manusia	— human being
perikemanusiaan	— humanitarianism
marah	— to be angry
memarahi	— to be angry at; scold
memarahkan	— to cause (X) to be angry

Mac	— March
mari	— let's, bye-bye; see you
masak	— something to do with cooking
memasak	— to cook
masalah	— (big) problem
masih	— still
masing-masing	— each
masuk	— to come in; enter
kemasukan	— possessed; infiltrated; entered
memasuki	— to enter (X)
memasukkan	— to make (X) enter; impor; put (in)
masyarakat	— society
mata	— eye
mati	— to die; be dead
kematian	— death; to suffer from the death of (C)
mahu	— to want; be willing to
kemahuan	— wish; desire; will
mawar	— rose
megah	— glorious; great
Mei	— May
meja	— table
meja makan	— dining table
Mekah	— Mecca
melainkan	— on the other hand; but
memang	— indeed
menang	— to be victorious; win
kemenangan	— victory
mendung	— to be cloudy
mengerti	— to understand
menteri	— minister (of States, etc.)
kementerian	— ministry
merah	— red

155

merdeka	— independent; free
kemerdekaan	— independence; freedom
mereka	— they; their; them
meskipun	— although
mesjid	— mosque
meter	— meter
milik	— property; something to do with owning
memiliki	— to own
pemilik	— owner
minggu	— week
Minggu	— Sunday
minta	— something to do with asking
meminta	— to ask for; request
permintaan	— (a) request
minum	— to drink
minuman	— (a) drink
minuman keras	— alcoholic drink
minyak	— oil
miskin	— poor (not rich)
modal	— capital
moden	— modern
moga-moga	— I/we hope; hopefully
mogok	— to break down; out of order; be on strike
mohon	— something to do with requesting
memohon	— to request (from lower to higher people)
permohonan	— (a) request (from lower to higher people)
mu	— short form for kamu
muda	— young
pemuda	— young man
mudah	— easy
mempermudah	— to make (X) easy;
mudah	— simplify

muka	— front; face
mulai	— to begin
memulai	— to begin (with person as subject)
mulut	— mouth
mungkin	— possible; may be
kemungkinan	— possibility
murah	— cheap
musik	— music
muzium	— museum
musuh	— enemy
mutlak	— absolute
mutu	— quality; standard
bermutu	— to have quality

– N –

nah	— well now
naik	— to ride; go up
menaiki	— to ride on; climb
menaikkan	— to raise
nakal	— naughty
nama	— name
bernama	— to be called/named
menamakan	— to name; label
nanti	— later (from present time)
nasihat	— advice
menasihati	— to advice
nasi	— cooked rice
nasib	— fate
nasional	— national
nasionalis	— nationalist

157

nasionalisme	— nationalism
naskah	— manuscript
negara	— country; state
negara yang sedang berkembang	— developing country
negara yang sudah maju	— developed country
negeri	— country; state
nikmat	— something to do with enjoying
menikmati	— to enjoy
nilai	— grade; value
nyanyi	— something to do with singing
menyanyi	— to sing
nyanyian	— song
nyata	— clear obvious
menyatakan perang	— to declare war on

– O –

oleh	— agentive marker
orang	— people; person
orang tua	— parents
seorang	— classifier for human beings
organisasi	— organization
orientasi	— orientation

– P –

padahal	— whereas
padat	— crowded; dense
padi	— rice plant

padu	— something to do with blending
berpadu	— blended
memadukan	— to blend (X and Y)
pemadu	— one who does the blending
perpaduan	— blend; fusion
pagar	— fence
pagi	— morning
selamat pagi	— good morning
pahat	— something to do with carving
memahat	— to carve
pemahat	— carve
pahlawan	— hero
pajak	— tax
pak	— short form for bapa something to do with packing
pakai	— something to do with using or wearing
memakai	— to use; wear
pakaian	— clothes
paket	— package; packet
paling	— most (beautiful, difficut etc.)
palsu	— false
kepalsuan	— falsity
memalsu	— to forge
pemalsuan	— forgery; falsification
paman	— uncle
pamer	— something to do with showing off
pameran	— exhibit
memamarkan	— to exhibit; show off
panas	— hot
kepanasan	— to suffer from the heat
pandai	— bright; smart; clever
panen	— harvest; to harvest

159

pengeran	— prince
panggil	— something to do with calling
memanggil	— to call; summon
memanggilkan	— to call; summon (for someone)
panggung	— stage (for shows —
panggung terbuka	— amphitheater
pangkat	— rank; power (in math)
panglima	— commander
panjang	— long (of measurement)
memanjangkan	— to lengthen
pantai	— beach; shore
pantas	— proper; appropriate
papan tulis	— blackboard
para	— plural form for collective humans
pasang	— something to do with installing
memasang	— to install
pasar	— market
pasar malam	— carnival; night fair
pastor	— Catholic priest
patung	— statue
payung	— umbrella
pecah	— broken; something to do with breaking or solving
memecah	— to break
memecahkan	— to break; solve
pecahan	— fraction; piece; offshoot; fragment
pemecahan	— (the) breaking/solving; solution
perpecahan	— split; dissension
pedas	— hot (of child peppers)
pegang	— something to do with holding
berpegang	— to stick (to)
memegang	— to hold

memegang peranan	— to play a role
pemegang	— holder
pegawai	— employee
pelan-pelan	— slow; slowly
pelopor	— pioneer
pen	— pen
pendapat	— opinion
pendek	— short
penduduk	— population; inhabitant
pengaruh	— influence
mempengaruhi	— to influence
pensel	— pencil
penting	— important
penuh (dengan)	— full (of)
perak	— informal form for rupiah
peranan	— role
perang	— war
berperang	— to wage war
menyatakan perang	— to declare war (on)
perangai	— attitude; behavior
percaya	— to believe; trust
mempercayai	— to trust (X)
peduli (amat)	— do not care
tidak peduli	— do not care
pergi	— to go
kepergian	— to departure
periksa	— something to do with examining or inspecting
memeriksa	— to examine inspect
pemeriksa	— examine inspector
pemeriksaan	— examination; inspection
perintah	— order

memerintah	— to rule; govern; give order
pemerintah	— government
pemerintahan	— government; administration
peristiwa	— affair; incident; even
perlu	— necessary
memerlukan	— to need
pernah	— ever; once (I lived in X etc.)
perpustakaan	— library
peratus	— percent
persis	— precise; precisely
pertama	— first
pertama-tama	— first of all
pesan	— something to do with ordering; (a) message
memesan	— to order books, etc.)
memesankan	— to order (for someone)
memesan tempat	— to book a seat
pesanan	— (an) order
pesta	— party
pidato	— speech
berpidato	— to delivery a speech
pikir	— something to do with thinking
memikirkan	— to think; give thought to
permikiran	— (the) thinking
pikiran	— thought
pilih	— something to do with choosing or selecting
memilih	— to choose; select; clect
memilihkan	— to choose; select; elect (for someone)
pemilihan	— selection; election
pemilihan umum	— general election
pimpin	— something to do with leading

memimpin	— to lead
pimpinan	— leader
pimpinan	— leadership
pinang	— something to do with marriage proposing
meminang	— to propose for marriage
pinangan	— marriage proposal
pincang	— crippled
pindah	— to move
kepindahan	— migration; move (to a place)
memindahkan	— to move (X)
memindahi	— to move (X) several times
pemindahan	— (the) moving; transfer
perindahan	— migration
pindahan	— something to do with secluding
pinjam	— something to do with borrowing
meminjam	— to borrow
meminjamkan	— to borrow (for someone); to lend
pintu	— door
piring	— plate (for food)
pisah	— something to do with separating
berpisah	— to be separated
memisah	— to separate (X)
pemisahan	— (the) separating
perpisahan	— (the) parting; farewell; separation
pohon	— tree
polis	— police
politik	— politics
sains politik	— political science
politikus	— politician
pos	— post
mengeposkan	to post/mail (letters)
peramugari	— stewardes

pria	— male; man
peribadi	— private
program	— programme
puasa	— something to do with fasting
berpuasa	— to fast
bulan puasa	— fasting month
puja	— something to do with worshipping
memuja	— to worship
pujaan	— idol; (X) that one worships
pemujaan	— (a) worship
pujangga	— man of letters
pukul	— o'clock; something to do with hitting
memukul	— to hit; strike
memukuli	— to hit; strike repeatedly
pulang	— to go home
memulangkan	— to send home
pulau	— island
kepulauan	— group of islands; archipelago
puluh	— unit of ten
pun	— even; too
puncak	— peak; top
punya	— to have; possess
kepunyaan	— property of; belong to
mempunyai	— to have; to possess
pupuk	— fertilizer
purbakala	— ancient; old
putih	— white
puteri	— girl of royal family; girl

– R –

radio	— radio
rahsia	— secret; (a) secret
raja	— king
kerajaan	— kingdom
merajai	— to rule (as a king)
rajin	— diligent
raksasa	— giant
ramah	— friendly
ramai	— noisy; lively; busy (not of work). bustling
ramal	— something to do with foretelling
meramalkan	— to foretell
ramalan	— prediction
rambut	— hair
rasa	— taste; feeling
merasa	— to feel
merasakan	— to taste
ratus	— unit of hundred
realisasi	— realization
merealisasi	— to make (X) into reality; realize
realistik	— realistic
renang	— something to do with swimming
berenang	— to swim
kolam renang	— swimming pool
rempah-rempah	— spices
rencana	— plan
merencanakan	— to plan
resmi	— official
meresmikan	— to make (X) official
restu	— (a) blessing
merestui	— to bless

revolusi	— revolution
ribu	— unit for a thousand
rintang	— something to do with hindering
rintangan	— hindrance; interperence obstacle
riwayat hidup	— biography
rokok	— cigarette
merokok	— to smoke
rokok kretek	— clove cigarette
roman	— (a) novel; romance
ruang	— space
ruang kuliah	— lecture hall
rugi	— to lose (money, etc.)
kerugian	— loss
merugikan	— to be disadvantageous to
rukun	— to be in harmony; teaching; foundation
rukun Islam	— Islamic teaching
rumah	— house
rumah makan	— restaurant
rumah sakit	— hospital
runding	— something to do with negotiating
perundingan	— negotiation
rupa	— face; look
merupakan	— constitute

– S –

sabun	— soap
sah	— leg 1; valid
saing	— something to do with rivaling
bersaing	— to be in competition; compete
menyaingi	— to rival; rival with

saingan	— competitor; rival; cimpetition
saja	— just; only
sakit	— to be sick
kesakitan	— to be in pain; suffer from pain
menyakiti	— to hurt
penyakit	— disease
sakti	— supernaturally powerful
kesaktian	— supernatural power
salah	— wrong; mistaken
menyalahkan	— to blame
salah satu	— one of the
salah seorang	— one of the (person)
salin	— something to do with copying
menyalin	— to copy
saling	— mutually; each other
salji	— snow
sama	— same
bersama	— together
sama dengan	— to equal
sama.... nya	— the same.... as
sambal	— chilly dish
sampai	— until; as far as; to reach
sampai bertemu lagi	— until (we) meet again
sana	— (over) there
di sana	— (at) over there
sangat	— very
sanggup	— to be able to; have the capabilities (to do X)
sangka	— something to do with suspecting
menyangka	— to suspect
sangkar	— nest

167

saran	— suggestion
	— scholar
sarjana	— lawyer
sastera	— literature
kesusasteraan	— literature
sate	— pieces of meat put in a skewer
satria	— knight
satu	— one
bersatu	— to be united
kesatuan	— unity
menyatukan	— to unite
penyatuan	— uniting; unification
persatuan	— union; associative
satu per satu	— one by one
saudara	— you; relative (brother, sister, etc.); Mr.
sawah	— padi field
saya	— I; me; my
sayang	— too bad, beloved
sayap	— wing
sayuran	— vegetable
se	— one (usually followed by a classifier)
sebab	— because
menyebabkan	— to cause
sebagai	— as (a soldier student, etc.)
sebelah	— side
sebelum	— before
sebenarnya	— actually; in fact
sebentar	— in a moment; for a short time
sedang	— in the process of
sedangkan	— whereas; while
sedap	— delicious; tasty
sederhana	— simple; modest

sedih	— to be sad
menyedihkan	— to be saddening; to sadden
segan	— to be reluctant; respectful
menyegani	— to respect
segar	— fresh
segera	— soon
segi	— side (political, scientific, etc.)
sihat	— healthy
kesihatan	— health
sehingga	— until
sejak	— since (temporal)
sejarah	— history
sekali	— very; very much
sekalian	— (you) all
sekarang	— now
sekolah	— school; to go to school
sekretari	— secretary
sektor	— sector
selama	— as long as (temporal and conditional)
selamat	— safe (of person)
selamat jalan	— Have a nice trip!; good bye
selamat malam	(said by the one staying)
selamat malam	— Good evening; good night
selamat pagi	— Good morning
selamat tengahari	— Good day
selamat tinggal	— Good-bye (said by the one leaving)
selalu	— always
selatan	— south
selesai	— to be over; finished
menyelesaikan	— to finish (X)
penyelesaian	— ending; solution
selidik	— something to do with investigating

169

menyelidiki	— to investigate
penyelidikan	— investigation
seluruh	— entire; whole
sembilan	— nine
sembahyang	— to pray
sementara	— temporary; temporarily
seminar	— seminar
sempat	— to have a chance
kesempatan	— (a) chance; opportunity
sempurna	— perfect
kesempurnaan	— perfection
menyempurnakan	— to perfect
penyempurnaan	— (the) perfecting
semua	— all
sen	— cent
sendiri	— alone
seni	— art
kesenian	— art
seniman	— artist
senjata	— weapon
senjata api	— firearms
sudu	— spoons
sengketa	— dispute
seperti	— like (this, that, etc.)
serah	— something to do with surrendering or delivering
menyerah	— to entrust (followed by the person entrusted)
menyerahkan	— to entrust (followed by the thing entrusted)
penyerah	
penyerahan	— (the) surrender; (the) take over; delivery
serang	— something to do with attacking

menyerang	— to attack
serangan	— (an) attack
sering	— often
seseorang	— someone
sesudah/setelah	— after
sesudah itu	— afterward
setan	— satan
stesen	— station (of trains buses, etc.)
setelah	— after
setengah	— half
setuju	— to agree
setuju dengan	— to agree with
menyetujui	— to agree with
persetujuan	— agreement
sewa	— rent
menyewa	— to rent; hire
menyewakan	— to rent out
sia-sia	— futile
siang	— day time
siap	— ready
siapa	— who; whom; whose
barang siapa	— whoever (followed by a verb)
siar	— something to do with broadcasting
menyiarkan	— to broadcast; announce; spread
siaran	— (a) broadcast
sibuk	— busy (of work, study, etc.)
kesibukan	— activity
sidang	— session; meeting
bersidang	— to have a session, meet
sifat	— characteristic
bersifat	— to have the characteristic of
sikap	— attitude

siksa	— something to do with torturing
menyiksa	— to torture
siksaan	— (a) torture
silakan	— please (come in, etc.)
simpan	— something to do with keeping
menyimpan	— to keep
menyimpankan	— to keep (for someone)
singgah	— to stop by/over; drop by
singkat	— something to do with stepping aside
menyingkir	— to step aside
menyingkiri	— to avoid
menyingkirkan	— to make to step aside eliminate
sini	— (over) there
siram	— something to do with watering
menyirami	— to sprinkle; water
situ	— over there (not too far)
situasi	— situation
soal	— case; matter; problem
persoalan	— case; matter; problem
tidak jadi soal	— it does not matter
sombong	— stuck up; arrogant
sosial	— social
suami	— husband
suara	— voice
sesuatu	— something
suci	— sacred; pure
kesucian	— purity sacredness
sudah	— already
suka	— to like
kesukaan	— what one likes; hobbies
menyukai	— to like
sukar	— difficult; hard

menyukari	— to make (X) more difficult
suku	— tribe; ethnic group
kesukuan	— ethnic (matters)
sumbang	— something to do with contributng
menyumbang	— to contribute
sumbangan	— contribution
sumpah	— pledge; promise
sungguh	— really; truly
supaya	— in order to
surat	— letter
menyurat	— to write a letter to
surat perjalanan	— travel document
surau	— neighbourhood mosque
suruh	— something to do with ordering
pesuruh	— messanger
susah	— difficult; complicuted
susul	— something to do with catching up
menyusul	— to atch up; join (later)
syair	— poem
penyair	— poet

– T –

tabung	— something to do with saving money
menabung	— to save
tabungan	— savings
tahan	— something to do with restraining, detaining, or defending
menahan	— to detain, imprison; retrain
penahanan	— arrest; detention
pertahanan	— defense

tahanan	— resistance; prisoner
tahu	— to know
tahun	— year
tajam	— sharp
menajamkan	— to sharpen
mempertajamkan	— to further sharpen
takut	— to be afraid
ketakutan	— to be scared
taman	— (a) park
tamat	— to end
tambah	— plus
tampar	— something to do with slapping
menampar	— to slap
menampari	— to slap repeatedly
tamu	— guest
tanam	— something to do with planting
menanamkan	— to plant
penanaman	— planting; investment
tertanam	— planted; implated
tandatangan	— signature
menandatangani	— to sign
tandus	— barren, not firtile
tanggal	— date (of month)
tanggungjawab	— responsible; responsibility
tangkap	— something to do with arresting or catching
menangkap	— to arrest; seize; catch
tani	— something to do with farming
petani	— farmer
pertanian	— farming; agriculture
tanpa	— without
tanya	— something to do with asking

bertanya	— to ask (questions, etc.)
pertanyaan	— (a) question
taraf	— level; stage
tari	— something to do with dancing
menari	— to dance
penari	— dancer
tari-tarian	— various dances
tarik	— something to do with attracting
menarik	— to pull; interest; be interesting
taruh	— something to do with putting
menaruhkan	— to put; place
tatausaha	— administration) of schools; universities, etc.)
tawar	— something to do with offering or bargaining
menawar	— to offer a price (in bargaining)
menawari	— to offer (followed by the person offered)
menawarkan	— to offer (followed by the thing offered)
tebal	— thick
teguh	— firm
teh	— tea
telinga	— ear
teliti	— careful; accurate; in detail; through
tema	— theme
teman	— friend
menemani	— to accompany; to keep company
tembak	— something to do with shooting
menambak	— to shoot
menembaki	— to shoot repeatedly
tembok	— wall
tempat	— (a) place
tempuh	— something to do with facing

175

menempuh	— to face (a problem, etc.); go through
tempur	— something to do with battling
pertempuran	— (a) battle
temu	— something to do with meeting or finding
bertemu	— to meet (by chance); bump into
menemui	— to go in order to meet
menemukan	— to find; discover
penemuan	— discovery; finding
pertemuan	— meeting; get-together
tenaga	— energy; power (as in man power)
tenang	— peaceful; calm
tentang	— about; on; something to do with opposing
menentang	— to oppose
tentera	— military
teori	— theory
tepat	— accurate; exact
menepati	— to fullfil; keep (a promise, etc.)
terbit	— something to do with publishing
menerbitkan	— to publish
terdiri dari	— to consist of
tergantung pada	— to depend on
terhadap	— toward; against
terima	— something to do with receiving or accepting
menerima	— to receive; accept
terima kasih	— thank you
terjadi	— to happen
terjemah	— something to do with translating
menterjemahkan	— to translate
penterjemah	— translator
penterjemahan	— translating

terjemahan	— translation
terkenal	— well-known; famous
terlalu	— too (big; wide. etc.)
terserah	— up to (you, him, etc.)
terus	— to keep (united, going, etc.)
terutama	— especially, primarily
tetap	— to remain (unchanged, united etc.)
tetapi	— but
tiap	— every
tiba	— to arrive
tiba-tiba	— suddenly; unexpectedly
tidak	— not; no
tidak jadi apa	— it does not matter
tidak ke mana-mana	— not to anywhere
tidur	— to sleep
meniduri	— to sleep on (X); make love to
menidurkan	— to put (X) to bed; lay (X) down
tidur sekejap	— to take a nap. (a) nap
tiga	— three
tikus	— mouse
timbal-balik	— matual; reciprocal
timbang	— something to do with weighing
penimbangan	— weighing
pertimbangan	— consideration. advice
timbangan	— scale
timbul	— to emerge
menimbulkan	— to bring about
timur	— east
tindas	— something to do with oppressing or suppressing
menindas	— to oppress

penindasan	— oppression; suppression
tinggal	— to live; stay
meninggal	— to die; pass away
meninggalkan	— to leave (X)
peninggalan	— rilic
tinggi	— high; tall
tipu	— somethingto do with deceiving or cheating
tertipu	— to be deceived or cheated
titik-tolak	— point of departure
tolak	— something to do with refusing
menolak	— to refuse; turn down
penolakan	— refusal; refusing
tolakan	— refusal
tolong	— do (me) a favour; something to do with helping
menolong	— to help
pertolongan	— help
tonton	— to go to see (movies, plays, etc.)
tradisi	— tradition
tua	— old
ketua	— chairman; chief; head
mengetuai	— to head
tuan	— you; Sir; Mr.
tugas	— duty; task
petugas	— one who is charged to do (X)
tugu	— monument (usually of pillar shapes)
Tuhan	— God
ketuhanan	— God Almighty
bertuhan	— to believe in God
tuju	— something to do with going toward
menuju	— to go toward; head

tujuan	— destination
tujuh	— seven
tukang	— one who is good at doing (lower type) work
tukar	— something to do with exchanging
menukarkan	— to exchange
tulis	— something to do with writing
menulis	— to write
menuliskan	— to write (for someone)
penulis	— author; writer
tulisan	— writing; article
tumpang	— something to do with riding
penumpang	— passanger
tunda	— something to do with postponing
tunggu	— something to do with waiting
menunggu	— to wait for
tunjuk	— something to do with showing
petunjuk	— guidance; guide (not a person
pertunjukan	— (a) show; performance
turun	— to go down; descend
menurun	— to lower down
menurunkan	— something to do with following
turut	— according to
menurut	— closed
tutup	— to close (X)
menutup	— something to do with changing
ubah	— to change
berubah	— to change (X)
merubah/ merubah/ mengubah	

– U –

udara	— weather; air
ujian	— examination (in schools); to take an exam
ukir	— something to do with carving
mengukir	— to carve
pengukir	— carver
ukiran	— carving; statue
ukur	— something to do with measuring
mengukur	— to measure
ukuran	— measurement
ulang tahun	— birthday; anniversary
umum	— general; public
mengumumkan	— announcement
umur	— age
undang	— something to do with inviting
mengundang	— invitation
undur	— something to do with moving back
mengundurkan	— to withdraw
mengundurkan diri	— to resign
untuk	— for
untung	— lucky; to gain profit
keuntungan	— profit
upacara	— ceremony
upah	— pay; commission; tip
urus	— something to do with taking care of
mengurus	— to take care of; arrange
menguruskan	— to take care of (for someone)
pengurus	— car taker; officer (of committees, organizations, etc.
urusan	— something to be taken care of; matter

180

usaha	— endeavour; attempt
berusaha	— to try; attempt; endeavour (followed by a noun or a clause)
mengusahakan	— act of trying
pengusahaan	
perusahaan	— enterprise
usang	— obsolete; worn out
usul	— proposal; suggestion
mengusulkan	— to propose
utama	— main
utara	— north

– V –

visa	— visa

– W –

wajib	— obliged
kewajiban	— obligation
waktu	— time; when (temporal)
wanita	— female; women; girl
warganegara	— citizen
waris	— something to do with inheriting
mewarisi	— to inherit
warisan	— inheritance
warna	— colour
wartawan	— journalist
waspada	— cautious; alert